Let's Talk About Your Health:
A Biblically Based Approach

GLENDA F. HODGES AND
HAROLD B. BETTON

authorHOUSE®

AuthorHouse™
1663 Liberty Drive
Bloomington, IN 47403
www.authorhouse.com
Phone: 1-800-839-8640

First published by AuthorHouse 5/27/2011

ISBN: 978-1-4634-0180-1 (e)
ISBN: 978-1-4634-0182-5 (dj)
ISBN: 978-1-4634-0181-8 (sc)

Library of Congress Control Number: 2011906508

Printed in the United States of America

Table of Contents

Dedication

Since we began our research in the area of spirituality and medicine back in 2006, it has been our desire to help members of the faith and medical communities understand the importance and benefit of "working together." Although the Spirituality and Medicine seminar series started at Howard University Hospital and College of Medicine in 1998 and have continued yearly since that time, our initial work, _Spirituality and Medicine: Can the Two Walk Together?_, was not published until March 2009. As a result of the yearly seminars, we had amassed a significant amount of research that helped us prepare a well developed manuscript.

Almost one year later, we concluded that we needed to provide a handbook that would help clergypersons integrate much of the scientific research contained in our first publication. Accordingly, in February 2010, we produced, _Translating Spirituality and Medicine in the Healing Professions_. This user-friendly pocket-manual has proven to be an excellent guide for bridging the gap between the two disciplines of spirituality and medicine and is definitely an "easy read."

Many of the persons we have encountered during the years of our research have provided "thank you" and "God bless you" to us on numerous occasions and have told us how meaningful our research has been to them. As Christian authors, we are always mindful of God's direction as we seek to do His will through our writing. This book, _Let's Talk About your Health: A Biblically Based Approach,_ is designed to provide an understanding of how we believe the word of God helps us live whole and healthy lives. Accordingly, we dedicate this publication to all of those persons who are willing to join hands with us and become better stewards over the bodies that have been entrusted into our care. To you we say, "trust in the Lord with all your heart and lean not to your own understanding; in all your ways, acknowledge Him and he shall direct your path." (Proverbs 3:5-6). We thank God for you and appreciate your companionship on this journey of ministry and medicine.

Glenda F. Hodges

Harold B. Betton

Foreword

This book represents the third in a series of three books that we have authored in the area of spirituality and medicine. In each instance, we have sought to bring a new tool to this ever expanding discipline. As a physician-pastor, Dr. Betton has used the word of God on numerous occasions in his medical practice. From bedside to bedside, there seems to always be an occasion to share God's word with a hospitalized person. As attorney-minister working as a hospital administrator, Dr. Hodges continues to find herself in situations where she is presenting the power of God to those who are physically challenged.

From time to time, we have all desired one compendium that is easily portable and available as a ready resource containing spiritually relevant advice, scripture and testimonies to support the patient in his/her hour of need. For this reason, we are proud to co-author this resource. It is designed to aid the pastor, layperson, physician, physician extender, hospital chaplain and others in the pastoral care ministry who are involved in the care of patients. This book is useful in any setting where individual ministry occurs. The topics discussed in this manuscript easily translate to a variety of situations and circumstances.

We have arranged the material in eight chapters that address pertinent aspects of care. The testimonial applications provided are compellingly refreshing and the scriptures are meaningful and targeted to address special interests. Because it is not our intention to exhaust the landscape of each topic, ample space is provided for reader inspired comments and scripture.

Preface

We recognize the importance of this material for all persons involved in the care of others, whether lay, clergy or physician. We believe that this material provides an invaluable resource for sometimes hard to initiate conversations regarding illness burden or maintenance of health.

As we stated earlier, in 2009, we offered _Spirituality and Medicine: Can the Two Walk Together_? This book was devoted to summarizing ten years of Howard University Hospital's Spirituality and Medicine seminar series. It explored the scientific and historical relevance of the spirituality and medicine connection. In 2010, we presented _Translating Spirituality and Medicine in the Healing Professions: A Physician-Clergy Handbook_. This book was written as a pocket manual for physicians and clergy who care for the daily needs of patients and parishioners. It also included several tools that are useful in this process.

At this point one may ask, "Why another book?" We believe that the spirituality and medicine landscape remains fertile and, as such, there is much more that needs to be shared. This resource is designed as a conversation initiator. It includes difficult circumstances that are often faced by those in the healing professions and it provides suggested scripture references with commentary and testimony to assist in navigating these troubling waters. It is an easy read and includes a comprehensive index. As Christian authors, we have written from this theological persuasion. It is our prayer that our readers will be blessed by this work and encouraged by its content.

Glenda F. Hodges
Harold B. Betton

Introduction

The onset of illness should not be the motivation to determine whether there is a connection between spirituality and health. Prevention of illness and maintenance of ones' temple (body) is extensively discussed in scripture. Likewise, the commencement of a crisis should not become necessary before one recognizes that God's will invites us to live abundant lives in Christ Jesus. In view of these conclusions, we have accepted the quest to investigate and present to others the scriptural warrants that promote health and wellness.

In _Spirituality and Medicine Can the Two Walk Together?_, several testimonies were presented that were designed to encourage and validate our research. While we recognize that no one will ever know the mind of God beyond the canon of scriptures, we decidedly argue that miracles in our lives provide evidence of God's providence. These miracles are equally as legitimate as any other belief construct. In _Translating Spirituality and Medicine in the Healing Professions_, we provided considerable tools for physicians and clergypersons for their use in interacting with patients and parishioners experiencing physical challenges.

This third monograph, in our series of manuals, is perhaps the most convenient of the three. It provides conversation-initiating tools useful for anyone believing in the power of God in the spirituality and medicine connection. How many times has one approached another who was physically suffering and was at a loss for words? How many times did you desire to quote an appropriate scripture elucidating a certain situation but was ill equipped to do so? How many times have you gone to the bedside of a person who may not have been physically conscious of your presence and wanted something to say that would minister to his or her soul?

The answer to the above questions is the raison d'être for this book. We seek to bridge this chasm between the individuals' myriad illness states and their respective desires to be comforted by God's word. The book provides ample space for its user to write notes and more scripture as well as observations that may be helpful in ministering to situations faced by persons who are experiencing the burdens of illness.

For purposes of consistency, each chapter devotes itself to the answer of a particular question, which is followed by an appropriate introduction to that question. Primarily, scripture quotations used are based on the NKJV (New King James Version) of the Bible; however, the KJV (King James Version) has been substituted in some instances in order to provide the appropriate context.

CHAPTER ONE

Health and Wellness: The Primacy of Health and the Prevention of Illness

Does God Require us to Keep our Bodies Healthy?

Jesus' clarification in John's Good Shepherd narrative summarizes this section.

> The thief does not come except to steal, and to kill and to destroy. I have come that they may have life, and that they may have it more abundantly. (John 10:10)

This passage from John's gospel defines two roles, one of Satan and the other of Christ. Clearly, the roles are very opposite from each other. Satan's role is to steal, kill and destroy life; Jesus came to give us eternal life. This abundant life promises more than we would ever require and is beyond what would ever be necessary for our wellbeing. It is also the desire of Jesus Christ that our lives be unrestricted regarding his love and care. Within this unfailing paradigm are health, wellness and prosperity. In this regard, III John 2 is illustrative: "Beloved, I wish above all things that thou mayest prosper and be in health, even as thy soul prospers."

In his discourse to the church at Corinth, Paul echoes a similar position.

> Do you not know that you are the temple of God and that

> the Spirit of God dwells in you? If any one defiles the temple of God, God will destroy him. For the temple of God is holy, which temple ye are. (I Corinthians 3:16-17)

In these verses, Paul suggests that the maintenance of the temple (body) is our responsibility and to do otherwise is tantamount to defiling it. Such contamination of the body would lead us away from holiness and the lifestyle that is pleasing unto God. Holiness requires that we be set aside for God's use. When this occurs, we demonstrate our consistency in the knowledge of God's word and willingness to obey Him.

It is important to recognize that everything God created within us was designed to work in harmony. In states of illness, our bodies are out of harmony and reflect a strained or broken state of being. While this state of brokenness may not emanate from any fault or misdeed on our part, we nonetheless remain comforted by God's word and confident of His will. This helps us to concentrate on using our best efforts to maintain the temple, even in the midst of periods of brokenness.

Consider the following scriptures that speak to us on the importance of adherence to God's word.

Question: What does the Bible promise through obedience to God?

> My son, do not forget my law,
> But let your heart keep my commands;
> For length of days and long life
> And peace they will add to you.
>
> Do not be wise in your own eyes;
> Fear the Lord and depart from evil.
> It will be health to your flesh
> And strength to your bones. (Proverbs 3:1-2, 7-8)

Question: How do words affect or reflect our temples' state?

>The mouth of the righteous is a well of life.
>Wisdom is found on the lips of him who has understanding.
>(Proverbs 10:11a; 13a)

>But the tongue of the wise promotes health. (Proverbs 12:18b)

>Pleasant words are like a honeycomb, sweetness to the soul and health to the bones. (Proverbs 16:24)

Question: Does the Bible connect health and a prospering soul?

>Beloved, I pray that you may prosper in all things and be in health, just as your soul prospers. (3 John 2)

Question: Can our actions impact my temples' promises of God?

We offer the following themes and companion scriptures for your consideration.

A. Managing problems or challenges

>Take firm hold of instruction, do not let go;
>Keep her, for she is your life.
>Do not enter the path of the wicked,
>And do not walk in the way of evil.
>Avoid it; do not travel by it;
>Turn away from it and pass on. (Proverbs:13-15)

>Trust in the Lord with all your heart,
>And lean not on your own understanding;
>In all your ways acknowledge Him,
>And He shall direct your paths.

Do not be wise in your own eyes;
Fear the Lord and depart from evil.
It will be health to your flesh,
And strength to your bones. (Proverbs 3:5-8)

A wholesome tongue is a tree of life,
But perverseness in it breaks the spirit. (Proverbs 15:4)

B. Maintaining confidence in the face of life's issues
Keep sound wisdom and discretion;
So they will be life to your soul
And grace to your neck.
Then you will walk safely in your way,
And your foot will not stumble.
When you lie down, you will not be afraid;
Yes, you will lie down and your sleep will be sweet.
Do not be afraid of sudden terror,
Nor of trouble from the wicked when it comes;
For the Lord will be your confidence,
And will keep your foot from being caught.
(Proverbs 3:21b-26)

C. Maintaining sound mental health
Commit your works to the Lord, and your thoughts will be
established. (Proverbs 16:3)

When a man's ways please the Lord,
He makes even his enemies to be at peace with him. (Proverbs
16:7)

He who heeds the word wisely will find good, And whoever
trusts in the Lord, happy is he. (Proverbs 16:20)

He who gets wisdom loves his own soul;
He who keeps understanding will find good. (Proverbs 19:8)

The fear of the Lord leads to life,
And he who has it will abide in satisfaction; He will not be
visited with evil. (Proverbs 19:23)

You will keep him in perfect peace,
Whose mind is stayed on You,
Because he trusts in You. (Isaiah 26:3)

Lord, You will establish peace for us,
For You have also done all our works in us. (Isaiah 26:12)

The work of righteousness will be peace,
And the effect of righteousness, quietness and assurance
forever. (Isaiah 32:17)

And it shall come to pass
That before they call, I will answer;
And while they are still speaking, I will hear. (Isaiah 65:24)

Be anxious for nothing, but In everything by prayer and
supplication, with thanksgiving, let our requests be made
known to God; and the peace of God, which surpasses all
understanding, will guard your hearts and minds through
Christ Jesus. (Philippians 4:6)

Nutrition and Temple Maintenance

Diet and nutrition are primary focal points in our lives. These subjects are also discussed in depth in the Bible. While some may fail to realize it, the Word of the Lord has provided many reference texts on the subject as well as many spiritually based eating plans. What is one to do? How is one to decide what is good or bad to eat? Does following a specific eating plan provide an assurance of optimum health?

These and many other questions are pervasive across the landscape of nutrition, often leaving the reader with more questions than answers. In order to fully address this topic, we must understand what the Bible conveys regarding nutrition and its implications of the same. In order to clearly explicate God's message in this regard, we have provided a complete discussion of the Jewish dietary laws found in Leviticus chapter 11 and we follow with a commentary on these provisions.

LEVITICUS CHAPTER 11

[1] And the LORD spake unto Moses and to Aaron, saying unto them,

[2] Speak unto the children of Israel, saying, These are the beasts which ye shall eat among all the beasts that are on the earth.

[3] Whatsoever parteth the hoof, and is clovenfooted, and cheweth the cud, among the beasts, that shall ye eat.

[4] Nevertheless these shall ye not eat of them that chew the cud, or of them that divide the hoof: as the camel, because he cheweth the cud, but divideth not the hoof; he is unclean unto you.

[5] And the coney,[1] because he cheweth the cud, but divideth not the hoof; he is unclean unto you.

[6] And the hare, because he cheweth the cud, but divideth not the hoof; he is unclean unto you.

[7] And the swine, though he divide the hoof, and be clovenfooted, yet he cheweth not the cud; he is unclean unto you.

[8] Of their flesh shall ye not eat, and their carcase shall ye not touch; they are unclean unto you.

[9] These shall ye eat of all that are in the waters: whatsoever hath fins and scales in the waters, in the seas, and in the rivers, them shall ye eat.

[10] And all that have not fins and scales in the seas,[2] and in the rivers, of all that move in the waters, and of any living thing which is in the waters, they shall be an abomination unto you:

[11] They shall be even an abomination unto you; ye shall not eat of their flesh, but ye shall have their carcasses in abomination.

[12] Whatsoever hath neither fins nor scales in the waters that shall be an abomination unto you.

[13] And these are they which ye shall have in abomination among the fowls; they shall not be eaten, they are an abomination: the eagle, and the ossifrage, and the ospray,

[14] And the vulture, and the kite after his kind;

[15] Every raven after his kind;

[16] And the owl, and the night hawk, and the cuckow, and the hawk after his kind,

---

1   A small west Asian and southern African animal that looks like a rabbit
2   Shellfish, amphibians, water mammals, sharks, eels, catfish are among those prohibited.

[17] And the little owl, and the cormorant, and the great owl,

[18] And the swan, and the pelican, and the gier eagle,

[19] And the stork, the heron after her kind, and the lapwing, and the bat.[3]

[20] All fowls that creep, going upon all four, shall be an abomination unto you.

[21] Yet these may ye eat of every flying creeping thing that goeth upon all four, which have legs above their feet, to leap withal upon the earth;

[22] Even these of them ye may eat; the locust after his kind, and the bald locust after his kind, and the beetle after his kind, and the grasshopper after his kind.

[23] But all other flying creeping things, which have four feet,[4] shall be an abomination unto you.

[24] And for these ye shall be unclean: whosoever toucheth the carcass of them shall be unclean until the even.

[25] And whosoever beareth ought of the carcass of them shall wash his clothes, and be unclean until the even.

[26] The carcasses of every beast which divideth the hoof, and is not clovenfooted, nor cheweth the cud, are unclean unto you: every one that toucheth them shall be unclean.

[27] And whatsoever goeth upon his paws, among all manner of beasts that go on all four, those are unclean unto you: whoso toucheth their carcass shall be unclean until the even.

[28] And he that beareth the carcass of them shall wash his clothes, and be unclean until the even: they are unclean unto you.

---

3   Predatory birds
4   rodents, reptiles, worms, and some insects

[29] These also shall be unclean unto you among the creeping things that creep upon the earth; the weasel, and the mouse, and the tortoise after his kind,

[30] And the ferret, and the chameleon, and the lizard, and the snail, and the mole.

[31] These are unclean to you among all that creep: whosoever doth touch them, when they be dead, shall be unclean until the even.

[32] And upon whatsoever any of them, when they are dead, doth fall, it shall be unclean; whether it be any vessel of wood, or raiment, or skin, or sack, whatsoever vessel it be, wherein any work is done, it must be put into water, and it shall be unclean until the even; so it shall be cleansed.

[33] And every earthen vessel, where into any of them falleth, whatsoever is in it shall be unclean; and ye shall break it.

[34] Of all meat which may be eaten, that on which such water cometh shall be unclean: and all drink that may be drunk in every such vessel shall be unclean.

[35] And everything whereupon any part of their carcass falleth shall be unclean; whether it be oven, or ranges for pots, they shall be broken down: for they are unclean, and shall be unclean unto you.

[36] Nevertheless a fountain or pit, wherein there is plenty of water, shall be clean: but that which toucheth their carcass shall be unclean.

[37] And if any parts of their carcass fall upon any sowing seed which is to be sown, it shall be clean.

[38] But if any water be put upon the seed, and any part of their carcass fall thereon, it shall be unclean unto you.

[39] And if any beast, of which ye may eat, die; he that toucheth the carcass thereof shall be unclean until the even.

[40] And he that eateth of the carcass of it shall wash his clothes, and be unclean until the even: he also that beareth the carcass of it shall wash his clothes, and be unclean until the even.

[41] And every creeping thing that creepeth upon the earth shall be an abomination; it shall not be eaten.

[42] Whatsoever goeth upon the belly, and whatsoever goeth upon all four, or whatsoever hath more feet among all creeping things that creep upon the earth, them ye shall not eat; for they are an abomination.

[43] Ye shall not make yourselves abominable with any creeping thing that creepeth, neither shall ye make yourselves unclean with them, that ye should be defiled thereby.

[44] For I am the LORD your God: ye shall therefore sanctify yourselves, and ye shall be holy; for I am holy: neither shall ye defile yourselves with any manner of creeping thing that creepeth upon the earth.

[45] For I am the LORD that bringeth you up out of the land of Egypt, to be your God: ye shall therefore be holy, for I am holy.

[46] This is the law of the beasts, and of the fowl, and of every living creature that moveth in the waters, and of every creature that creepeth upon the earth:

[47] To make a difference between the unclean and the clean, and between the beast that may be eaten and the beast that may not be eaten. (KJV)

The dietary laws in Leviticus provide no explanation for the exclusion of certain animals in one's diet; however, they are clearly the recommended eating plan for the chosen of God, the emancipated children from Egypt. These descendants of Abraham were to be separated unto God and unique in dietary and worship styles. While a discussion of the dietary laws of other nations in the ancient Near East is not the purpose or intent of this book; we do recognize that dietary restrictions in other areas may have been influenced by those nations' eating and patterns of worship. Many persons have concluded that we should conform our diets and eating plans to that of Daniel. Rather than omit this area of discussion, we present our material by asking the following direct question.

Does the Bible teach that we follow Daniel's eating plan by consuming vegetables and only drinking water?

> [5] And the king appointed them a daily provision of the king's meat, and of the wine which he drank: so nourishing them three years, that at the end thereof they might stand before the king.
>
> [6] Now among these were of the children of Judah, Daniel, Hananiah, Mishael, and Azariah:
>
> [7] Unto whom the prince of the eunuchs gave names: for he gave unto Daniel the name of Belteshazzar; and to Hananiah, of Shadrach; and to Mishael, of Meshach; and to Azariah, of Abed-nego.
>
> [11] Then said Daniel to Melzar, whom the prince of the eunuchs had set over Daniel, Hananiah, Mishael, and Azariah,

[12] Prove thy servants, I beseech thee, ten days; and let them give us pulse[5] to eat, and water to drink.

[13] Then let our countenances be looked upon before thee, and the countenance of the children that eat of the portion of the king's meat: and as thou seest, deal with thy servants. (Daniel 1:5-7, 11-13 KJV)

The scripture suggests that Daniel's diet presented a problem for the King. Daniel chose foods that would sustain him because he relied upon God to maintain his temple. Daniel's choice of foods was more restrictive than the diet offered under the Jewish law of permissible foods. His diet represented a personal choice that constituted a fast to prove who was in charge of the countenance and appearance of his (Daniel's) body (temple).

There is also much discussion around the notion of extending one's nutritional intake to exceed that of Jewish teachings. In embracing this topic, we offer the following question:

Can one interpret Peter's vision as God's permission to eat outside of the Jewish dietary restrictions?

[11] And I saw heaven opened, and a certain vessel descending unto him, as it had been a great sheet knit at the four corners, and let down to the earth:

[12] Wherein were all manner of four-footed beasts of the earth, and wild beasts, and creeping things, and fowls of the air.

[13] And there came a voice to him, Rise, Peter; kill, and eat.

[14] But Peter said, not so, Lord; for I have never eaten anything that is common or unclean.

---

5   Vegetables

> [15] And the voice spake unto him again the second time, what God hath cleansed, that call not thou common. (Acts 10:11-15, KJV)

These Scriptures serve as an argument against racial discrimination in the dispensation of God's grace. Peter was to go to the home of a Gentile, Cornelius, and present the plan of salvation. Under ordinary circumstances, Peter would never have associated with a Gentile; however, through this vision, God lets him know that nothing he made was unclean.

Our examination suggests that the Gentiles' acceptance of Christ had fewer dietary restrictions, as noted in the letter to Antioch after the first Jerusalem Council.

> [28] For it seemed good to the Holy Ghost, and to us, to lay upon you no greater burden than these necessary things;
> [29] That ye abstain from meats offered to idols, and from blood, and from things strangled, and from fornication: from which if ye keep yourselves, ye shall do well. Fare ye well. (Acts 15:28-29,KJV)

At first glance, one might consider this a bit confusing and even inconsistent. Further examination of the scriptures reveals both the letter and the spirit of the law.
How did Paul clarify the issue?

> [4] For every creature of God is good, and nothing to be refused, if it be received with thanksgiving:
> [5] For it is sanctified by the word of God and prayer. (1 Timothy 4:4-5, KJV)

As is apparent to the writers, much attention is often placed on restrictions in God's word, rather than on the outcome that God desires as a result of compliance with His word. While these discussions clearly provide rich "food for thought," we conclude that it is not necessarily the dietary law(s) that explain and define godly nutrition, but rather restraint, holiness and obedience.

What then can we conclude to be nutrition?

Nutrition can be defined as that content of food (solid and liquid) sustenance that keeps our bodies functioning in harmony. Accordingly, nutrition is nuanced by a variety of content rather than that which is merely defined as prescribed menu. While it is not our intention to offer any particular diet or eating plan, we are resolved that anything that defiles the temple may lead to its destruction. Irresponsible eating, unmonitored eating leading to obesity, worsening disease states, anorexic states or anything that upsets the harmony of our bodies falls outside of God's will and is therefore inconsistent with God's plan of nutrition for our lives. Recognition of this fact is key to answering our initial set of questions. What is one to do? How is one to decide what is good or bad to eat? Does following a specific plan assure one of good health? We recommend that all persons suffering from any chronic illnesses consult their physician(s). For maintenance of optimal health, we recommend the following:[6]

Control your portion sizes

Use smaller plates with ½ of the plate filled with vegetables and salad or you might consider one serving of carbohydrate (bread or a starchy vegetable such as corn or potato) and one helping of protein (beans or meat).

---

6   This information is taken directly from a pamphlet entitled *Healthy Choices*, authored by Dr. Betton and given to his patients suffering from chronic illnesses. The information found within this pamphlet is consistent with the benefits of that diet eaten by the 3 Hebrews boys of Daniel Chapter one.

<u>Always include fiber</u>

Consume healthy portions of fruits and nuts but beware of bananas, grapes and melons because of their sugar content. If possible, include a piece of fruit with each meal. Apples, oranges, and berries are excellent choices. Consider choosing raw vegetables as occasional snacks. They are great sources of vitamins and minerals and are very portable.

<u>Guard against fatty substances</u>

Use unsaturated fats such as canola or olive oil. Avoid butter, Crisco, lard, or vegetable oil. Refrain from cooking vegetables in pork products. Smoked turkey is an excellent, healthy option for pork. Trans fat (a common name for unsaturated fat) is bad for you! Trans fat may be monounsaturated or polyunsaturated. In this regard, we offer the following website for helpful information.

A. www.acaloriecounter.com/fast-food-trans-fat.php (Discusses the eighty-eight fast foods that are highest in trans fats).

B. www.cspinet.org/nah/6_99/transfat3.html (Explains how to avoid trans-fat when dining out)

C. lowfatcooking.about/com/od/healthandfitness/p/transfats.htm (Discusses what you need to know about trans fats of fatty acids)

Studies show that unsaturated fat tends to raise your cholesterol levels and may add unwanted pounds. We recommend that you avoid foods containing hydrogenated oil or those that list liquid oil as the first ingredient. In order to consolidate the information that we believe to be helpful to you in this category, we offer the following "less than healthy" food choices and offer the following "good for you" substitutes.

INSTEAD OF THESE	TRY THESE
High fat meats	Trimmed or lean meat
Ice cream	Sherbet or low fat ice cream
Jelly, jam, syrups	Fruit spreads
Mayonnaise	Low-fat Mayonnaise
Pork chops	Pork Tenderloin[7]
Sour cream	Yogurt, fat free sour cream
Tuna packed in oil	Tuna packed in water
Whole milk	Non-fat or 2% milk

---

7   No meat was included in the diet consumed by the young men of Daniel Chapter one. Instead of Pork one could include a meat consistent with the Jewish diet if desired but portion size should be limited to 4 ounces. Tuna is permissible on the Jewish diet.

TESTIMONIAL APPLICATION
The Story of Rev. W.
(as told by Dr. Betton)

If one looks across the landscape of wonderful patients, one will stand out as a testimonial to the truths written in this chapter. Such is the case with Rev. W., an 85-year-old, Church of Christ pastor whose daily mission is to exercise, eat responsibly and keep his blood pressure under control. Rev. W. was not always a practitioner of these teachings. Like so many clergymen, he experienced his days of careless consumption and couch cradling comforts. When he was diagnosed with prostate cancer, he had a wakeup call. Rev. W. was now an obese, poorly controlled hypertensive, prostate cancer patient in need of spiritual and medical help. I met him at this time and we charted a plan of attack.

Rev. W. was sent to a good urologist and was able to get his prostate cancer managed. The church nurse kept up with his blood pressure readings, recorded them and reminded him to take his vital signs log to each office appointment. His blood pressure medications were adjusted according to his out-of-office numbers because he suffered from an even higher blood pressure when in the medical office. His prostate cancer went into remission and all indicators of disease remained absent. Rev. W lives within close proximity to a 24-hour health center, conducive for "exercising at your leisure." Never one to mind early rising, Rev W would frequently come to the office for his 7:00 am appointments with a smile on his face reporting that he had been up since 3:00am. Before arriving at the office, he had sometimes already completed 4 miles on the treadmill.

At the time of this writing, Rev W no longer depends on out-of-office blood pressure measurements as a control measure. He continues to walk and watch his diet. He is no longer obese. His average blood pressure remains 130/80, weight 160, and he is cancer-free. This is the story of an aged preacher whose present daily activities include meditation, nutrition, exercise and care of his body. He continues to come into my office with a smile on his face and praises emanating from his lips for what God has done in his life!

CHAPTER TWO

Health and Wellness: The Restorative Power of Meditation and Prayer

Does Prayer Really Work?

Prayer is one of the major teachings of scripture; it allows us to communicate with our creator and rest in His provisions for our lives. We are instructed to always pray (Luke 11:2; 18:1; 1 Thess. 5:17) with confidence (John 14:13-14, Mark 11:23-24, 1 John 5:14-15, Heb 4:16) recognizing that God hears and attends to our cry (Isaiah 65:24). We are instructed to pray for one another for healing (James 5:16), to avoid temptation (Matthew 26:41), for God's will in our lives (Job 42:8; Jeremiah 42:2; 2 Thessalonians 3:1) and for those that afflict us (Matthew 5:44). Just as Christ prayed for us, (John 17) we should likewise pray for others in general and specific matters.

In prayer, there are certain requirements that must be met. First, we must know to whom our prayers are directed (Psalms 5:2; Isaiah 45:20; Matthew 6:6; Luke 10:2; 11:2; John 14:16). Secondly, we must approach Him with boldness (1 John 5:14-15, Hebrews 4:16). Finally, we must come with assurance of God's provisions as promised to us (Isaiah 65:24; John 14:13-14; Mark 11:23-24). In the background of prayer, the one who is praying must submit to the knowledge and belief that God is all in all (Ecclesiastes 3:14) and that His will is done in our lives. (1 John 2:16)

It is our belief that prayer changes things and it changes the one who is praying. As such, it is important to share these scriptures with others when speaking about prayer and its power. For these reasons, we provide additional axioms with the hope that they will encourage you to continue to pray without ceasing.

We are instructed to always pray.

And he said unto them, when ye pray, say, Our Father which art in heaven, Hallowed be thy name. Thy kingdom come. Thy will be done, as in heaven, so in earth. (Luke 11:2) And he spake a parable unto them to this end, that men ought always to pray and not to faint (Luke 18:1). One needs only to singularly experience the power of God through prayer in order to realize the importance of constant communication with Him.

Pray without ceasing.

1Thessalonians 5:17 suggest that we pray constantly, in good times and in bad. Additionally, we must pray with confidence and in the name of Jesus. In order to enhance your prayer life, we offer the following scriptures for your consideration.

> And whatsoever ye shall ask in my name, that will I do, that the Father may be glorified in the Son. If ye shall ask any thing in my name, I will do it. (John 14:13-14)

> For verily I say unto you, That whosoever shall say unto this mountain, Be thou removed, and be thou cast into the sea; and shall not doubt in his heart, but shall believe that those things which he saith shall come to pass; he shall have whatsoever he saith. Therefore I say unto you, "What things soever ye desire,

when ye pray, believe that ye receive them, and ye shall have them." (Mark 11:23-24)

And this is the confidence that we have in him, that, if we ask any thing according to his will, he heareth us.

And if we know that he hears us, whatsoever we ask, we know that we have the petitions that we desired of him. (1 John 5:14-15)

Let us therefore come boldly unto the throne of grace that we may obtain mercy and find grace to help in time of need. (Hebrews 4:16)

We should recognize that God knows our situations and will answer our prayers.

And it shall come to pass, that before they call, I will answer; and while they are yet speaking, I will hear. (Isaiah 65:24)

We are instructed to pray for one another.

Confess your faults one to another and pray one for another, that ye may be healed. The effectual, fervent prayer of a righteous man availeth much. (James 5:16)

We are to pray to avoid entering into temptation.

Watch and pray, that ye enter not into temptation: the spirit indeed is willing, but the flesh is weak. (Matthew 26:41)

We are to pray for God's will to be manifested in our lives.

Therefore take unto you now seven bullocks and seven rams, and go to my servant Job and offer up for yourselves a burnt offering; and my servant Job shall pray for you: for him will I accept: lest I deal with you after your folly, in that ye have not spoken of me the thing which is right, like my servant Job. (Job 42:8)

And he said unto Jeremiah the prophet, Let me beseech thee, our supplication be accepted before thee, and pray for us unto the LORD thy God, even for all this remnant; for we are left but a few of many, as thine eyes do behold us. (Jeremiah 42:2)

Finally, brethren, pray for us, that the word of the Lord may have free course, and be glorified, even as it is with you: (2 Thessalonians 3:1)

We are to pray for those that afflict us.

But I say unto you, Love your enemies, bless them that curse you, do good to them that hate you, and pray for them which despitefully use you, and persecute you. (Matthew 5:44)

Meditation: Pondering God's word in your heart for restoration and maintenance of the temple.

In the 13th Howard University Hospital Spirituality and Medicine Seminar Series, meditation was discussed as a tool to eliminate confusion and restore calm in our lives. Each person attending the meditation session was taught how to meditate. We have reproduced the technique here in its entirety.[8]

First, take a strong posture, sitting either cross-legged on a cushion on the floor, or in a chair, which supports an upright position. It is important that you support yourself: you are not leaning back. Hands are placed palms down on your thighs in a relaxed manner. Spine is upright, and the chest and heart area are open. Shoulders are slightly back yet relaxed and the head is slightly tilted down. Eyes are open and the gaze is lowered and placed about 5 feet in front of you in a

---

8   Jonathan Kirkendall, *Meditation: Eliminating Confusion and Restoring Calm*, Proceedings, 13th Annual Spirituality and Medicine Seminar Series. "Restoring the Temple" (Washington, D.C.: Howard University College of Medicine, 2010). 18-19.

soft position (i.e. you're not finding a spot on the floor and staring at that one spot; that will tire your eyes). Breathe in a normal fashion. There is no need to manipulate the breath. If you tend to grind your teeth, part your lips slightly – this will help to relax your jaw.

Once you have the posture, FEEL your body. Feel the strength and stability of this posture. The mind actually follows the body. The more stable and strong your posture, the more stable and strong your mind will be.

Breathe in a normal fashion, become aware of both the in-breath and the out-breath. Be aware of the sensation of the breath as it enters your nose, then let your awareness follow the breath down into your lungs. Feel your abdomen and your chest expand, then follow the breath out as you exhale. Let your mind continue to follow your breath in and out, in and out.

Do this for at least 5 minutes, extending the amount of time as you can tolerate.

Scripture has much to say about meditation. Consider the following Bible verses that we have included as you embrace the concept of meditating. When doing God's will for his life, Isaac went out in a field to meditate.

[63] And Isaac went out to meditate in the field at the eventide: and he lifted up his eyes, and saw, and, behold, the camels were coming. (Genesis 24:63)

God commanded Joshua to meditate on His book of the law day and night. This commandment was given before Joshua crossed the Jordan to start the conquest of Canaan.

[8] This book of the law shall not depart out of thy mouth; but thou shalt meditate therein day and night, that thou mayest observe to do according to all that is written therein: for then

thou shalt make thy way prosperous, and then thou shalt have good success. (Joshua 1:8)

The Psalmist lists meditation as one of the attributes of a blessed man, according to the law of God.

[1] Blessed is the man that walketh not in the counsel of the ungodly, nor standeth in the way of sinners, nor sitteth in the seat of the scornful.

[2] But his delight is in the law of the LORD; and in his law doth he meditate day and night (Psalm 1:1-2)

The Psalmist prays about the quality of the meditation.

Let the words of my mouth and the meditation of my heart be acceptable in your sight,

O Lord, my strength and redeemer. (Psalm 19:14)

Oh, how I love your law!

It is my meditation all the day. (Psalm 119:97)

Paul instructed Timothy to meditate on things taught to him. He admonished Timothy to meditate on those things and to give himself entirely to them in order that his progress would be seen by all who observed him. (1Timothy 4:15)

In each of these scriptures, to meditate means to ponder, speak to one's self and to carefully attend to that which is the subject of one's meditation. In these instances, the one meditating is not engaged in oral speech, but rather speech from within.

TESTIMONIAL APPLICATION
The Story of Bishop Gregory G. M. Ingram
118th Elected and Consecrated Bishop of
the African Methodist Episcopal Church

It is within a state of continual prayer that much about God is realized. While we may not completely know the mind of God, we are confident of the fact that He desires that we obey His word. In 2003, while serving the African Methodist Episcopal Church (AMEC) in Capetown, South Africa, Bishop Gregory G. M. Ingram, 118th elected and consecrated Bishop of the AMEC, was involved in a terrible automobile accident. Unfortunately, Bishop Ingram's driver lost his life in the accident; however, God spared the life of Bishop Ingram. During his sermon on April 15, 2010 at the Ecumenical Worship Service, as part of the 13th annual Spirituality and Medicine Seminar Series, Bishop Ingram boldly proclaimed the power of God to heal and restore one's body, mind and spirit. We present his testimony here as an indication of how faith in God and dependence on His word can change the outcome of a situation. Bishop Ingram describes his end result from the car accident as "sixteen miracles."

Sixteen Miracles from Bishop Ingram's Car Accident

I will never forget the automobile accident in South Africa on May 10, 2003, that took the life of my driver, David Van Neel and nearly took mine. I am here today because of the power and grace of God. I am a witness that "man's extremity is only God's opportunity." Sometimes we do not know why we are chosen to endure things that are not so pleasant; however, I have learned that "it was good that I was afflicted." The scriptures indicate that the righteous will inevitably suffer many afflictions; however, "God is able to deliver us out of them all." Following my crash, I experienced at least sixteen miracles that were indicative of the mighty hand of God moving in and through my body. I have detailed them as follows:

A. I did not die.

B. I did not bleed to death.

C. Despite severe trauma, I was able to maintain consciousness.

D. The broken ribs I suffered did not puncture my lungs.

E. Despite major damage, I maintained flexibility in my right wrist.

F. My skull was not crushed.

G. Though crushed like a tin can, the car did not explode.

H. Because I was wearing a clerical collar, the seatbelt did not sever my neck.

I. Although hanging by only a few tendons, my foot was saved.

J. I survived being transported to three hospitals in one night.

K. Gangrene did not set in, despite the fact that surgery to my right foot was delayed nearly ten hours after the accident.

L. I was spared having my foot amputated at the second hospital because the doctors were unable to move my clerical collar.

M. My cell phone survived the accident, enabling me to call my administrative assistant for help in rescuing me from the second hospital.

N. I avoided infection, despite three surgeries in seven days.

O. An orthopedic specialist and an anesthetist were found early the following morning when neither was supposed to be available.

P. God provided two caregivers, a man and his wife, to clean and dress my wounds each day for several weeks, which helped the open wounds on my foot to slowly heal.

On May 10, 2003 and the days that followed, God turned tragedy into triumph. Though I will limp for the rest of my life and bear the physical, mental and emotional scars of that accident until God calls me home, I still have a reason to rejoice. I am convinced that it was God who snatched me from the ferocious grip of death and restored my temple to a state of wholeness and wellness. While physicians are trained to accomplish astounding feats because of their medical acumen, only God is able to heal. Each day that I see the sun rise again or hear a bird chirping or experience any of the magnificent bounties of nature, I thank God that I was afflicted. Today, I am stronger; I am better; I am wiser and most importantly, I am closer to God. More than ever before, I have affirmed that I will follow the Lord for the rest of my life. I will also let my voice be heard to others that I encounter so that they will know that the God that I serve is indeed, able!

CHAPTER THREE

Coping with Life's Challenges

Does Faith in God Enable One to Cope with Illness?

If we conclude that God superintends our lives from birth to His return, then we must accept the fact the He understands all about us, even those twists and turns that are not so pleasant. Scripture supports this conclusion. The prophet Isaiah presents the following summation:

> And it shall come to pass that before they call I will answer and while they are yet speaking I will hear. (Isaiah 65:24)

When we counsel others, we are generally quick to tell them to accept God's will; we often encourage them to pray and meditate on His word and indeed, we encourage them to speak to their Pastor or spiritual advisor. How often do we practice the same thing? Do we approach life in a way that prepares us for its uncertainties? This chapter is devoted to a multitude of questions that deal with life's twists and turns and how to cope with them. We begin this chapter with basic information regarding exercise and diet. We follow with issues involving mental health, family illness, chronic illnesses, hospice and terminal illness. Where suitable, testimonies are offered as support for points that have been previously raised.

Did God create a natural mood elevating substance that improves our outlook?[9] People with a regular exercise schedule generally have a better outlook on life, are happier and feel better than those who "take to the couch." There is an explanation for this. Without citing every publication that supports this conclusion, it has been proven that exercise, depending upon the intensity, type and duration, causes a gland found within the brain (pituitary) to release chemicals called beta-endorphin and adrenocorticotrophin hormone (ACTH) which causes the adrenal gland to secrete cortisol. Physical exercise is now used to treat a multitude of mental health issues such as depression, tension, fatigue, anxiety and anger. It has also been found to enhance coping and in some cases, reduce or eliminate part or all of the symptoms of these problems. Scripture does not devote itself toward proving this scientific fact; however, much is written in the scriptures regarding care of one's temple. The following verses are illustrative:

> Do you not know that you are the temple of God and that the Spirit of God dwells in you? If anyone defiles the temple of God, God will destroy him. For the temple of God is holy, which temple you are. (1Corinthians 3:16-17)

It is the care of one's temple, both spiritually and biologically, that is important and this scripture provides evidence supporting the necessity of keeping one's temple as fit as possible. As one adopts a principle for healthy living, it is important to remember that exercise and a well balanced diet complement each other. Chapter one was devoted to a discussion of this important union.

Consistent with the importance of the maintenance of excellent

---

9   A. H. Goldfarb and A. Z. Jamurtas, "Beta-Endorphin response to Exercise. An update," Sports Medicine 1997; Jul; 24 (1):8-16. F. Fraioli, C. Moretti, et. al., "Physical exercise stimulates marked concomitant release of Beta-endorphin and adrenocorticotropic hormone (ACTS) in peripheral blood in man," Clinica Medica V, 15 October 1979. http://resources.metapress.com/pdf.

physical health is the requirement for mental well being. We include several scriptures which are helpful in understanding the importance of mental well being. Some researchers have suggested that prayer and meditation have significant positive effects on the body's ability to reach a seeming state of calmness. Likewise, one could suggest that one's cognizance and appreciation of a supreme being could also have a similar effect on an individual's mental soundness and health. We present the following questions and provide complementary scriptures that may be useful in considering answers for the questions we ask. Does reverencing God set the stage for mental tranquility?

The fear of the Lord is the beginning of wisdom,
and the knowledge of the Holy One is understanding. For by me your days will be multiplied, and the years of life will be added to you. (Proverbs 9:10-11)

The righteous should choose his friends carefully,
For the way of the wicked leads them astray. (Proverbs 12:26)

Where there is no counsel, the people fall;
But in the multitude of counselors there is safety. (Proverbs 11:14)

For you formed my inward parts;
You covered me in my mother's womb.
I will praise you, for I am fearfully and wonderfully made;
Marvelous are your works,
And that my soul knows very well.
My frame was not hidden from you,
When I was made in secret,

And skillfully wrought in the lowest parts of the earth. Your eyes saw my substance, being yet unformed. (Psalm 139:13-16)

You will keep him in perfect peace,
Whose mind is stayed on You,
Because he trusts in You. (Isaiah 26:3)

The work of righteousness will be peace,
And the effect of righteousness quietness and assurance forever. (Isaiah 32:17)

Does walking by God's statutes create happiness and assure mental stability?

Blessed is the man who walks not in the counsel of the ungodly,
Nor stands in the path of sinners,
Nor sits in the seat of the scornful;
But his delight is in the law of the Lord,
And in His law he meditates day and night.
He shall be like a tree
Planted by the rivers of water,
That brings forth its fruit in its season,
Whose leaf also shall not wither.
And whatever he does shall prosper.(Psalm 1:1-3)

Blessed are the poor in spirit, for theirs is the kingdom of heaven.
Blessed are those who mourn, for they shall be comforted.
Blessed are the meek, for they shall inherit the earth.

Blessed are those who hunger and thirst for righteousness, for they shall be filled.

Blessed are the merciful, for they shall obtain mercy.

Blessed are the pure in heart, for they shall see God.

Blessed are the peacemakers, for they shall be called sons of God.

Blessed are those who are persecuted for righteousness' sake, for theirs is the kingdom of God.

Blessed are you when they revile and persecute you, and say all kinds of evil against you falsely for my sake. (Matthew 5:1-11)

If you love God and He is the object of your faith, should one live a life filled with anxiety (distractions)?

Be anxious for nothing, but in everything by prayer and supplication, with thanksgiving, let your requests be made known to God;

And the peace of God, which surpasses all understanding, will guard your hearts and minds through Christ Jesus. (Philippians 4:6-7)

And Jesus answered and said to her, "Martha, Martha, you are worried and troubled about many things. But one thing is needed, and Mary has chosen that good part, which will not be taken away from her." (Luke 10:41-42)

Sometimes it is difficult to cope with illness due to family and interpersonal concerns; what instruction does God provide?

Scripture clearly lets us know that man is born to die and as such, will be faced with illness. The Gospel narratives are replete with healing stories. Illness was pervasive and difficult for many to endure without faith. Consider the following examples from the ministry of Jesus:

In Faith:

> When Jesus saw him lying there, and knew that he already had been in that condition a long time, he said to him, "Do you want to be made well?"
>
> The sick man answered Him, "Sir, I have no man to put me into the pool when the water is stirred up; but while I am coming, another steps down before me." Jesus said to him, "Rise, take up your bed and walk." And immediately the man was made well, took up his bed, and walked.
> (John 5:6-9)

> Now it happened on the next day, when they had come down from the mountain, that a great multitude met Him. Suddenly a man from the multitude cried out, saying, "Teacher, I implore you, look on my son, for he is my only child. And behold a spirit seizes him, and he suddenly cries out; it convulses him so that he foams at the mouth; and it departs from him with great difficulty, bruising him. So I implored your disciples to cast it out, but they could not." Then Jesus answered and said, "O faithless and perverse generation, how long shall I be with you and bear with you? Bring your son here." And as he was still coming, the demon threw him down and convulsed him. Then Jesus rebuked the unclean spirit, healed the child, and gave him back to his father.
> (Luke 9:37-42)

> Now a certain woman had a flow of blood for twelve years, and had suffered many things from many physicians. She

had spent all that she had and was no better, but rather grew worse. When she heard about Jesus, she came behind Him in the crowd and touched His garment. For she said, "If only I may touch His clothes, I shall be made well." Immediately the fountain of her blood was dried up, and she felt in her body that she was healed of the affliction. And Jesus, immediately knowing in Himself that power had gone out of Him, turned around in the crowd and said, "Who touched my clothes?"...And He said to her, "Daughter, your faith has made you well. Go in peace, and be healed of your affliction." (Mark 5:25-30, 34)

With Thanksgiving

Now they came to Jericho. As He went out of Jericho with His disciples and a great multitude, blind Bartimaeus, the son of Timaeus, sat by the road begging. And when he heard that it was Jesus of Nazareth, he began to cry out and say, "Jesus, Son of David, have mercy on me!"...So Jesus stood still and commanded him to be called. Then they called the blind man, saying to him, "Be of good cheer. Rise, He is calling you."... so Jesus answered and said to him, "What do you want Me to do for you?" The blind man said to Him, "Rabboni, that I may receive my sight." Then Jesus said to him, "Go your way; your faith has made you well." And immediately he received his sight and followed Jesus on the road. (Mark 10:46-49, 52)

Then they came to the other side of the sea, to the country of the Gadarenes. And when He had come out of the boat, immediately there met Him out of the tombs a man with an unclean spirit...When he saw Jesus from afar, he ran and worshiped Him. And he cried out with a loud voice and said,

"What have I to do with You, Jesus, son of the Most High God? I implore You by God that You do not torment me." For He said to him, "come out of the man, unclean spirit!" Then He asked him, "what is your name?"…And when He got into the boat, he who had been demon-possessed begged Him that he might be with Him. However, Jesus did not permit him, but said to him, "Go home to your friends, and tell them what great things the Lord has done for you, and how He has had compassion on you."

(Mark 5:1-2, 6-8, 18-19)

With Praise:

Now it happened as He went to Jerusalem that He passed through the midst of Samaria and Galilee. Then as He entered a certain village, there met him ten men who were lepers, who stood afar off. And they lifted up their voices and said, "Jesus, Master, have mercy on us!" So when He saw them, He said to them, "Go, show yourselves to the priests." And so it was that as they went, they were cleansed. And one of them, when he saw that he was healed, returned, and with a loud voice glorified God, and fell down on his face at His feet, giving him thanks, and he was a Samaritan. So Jesus answered and said, "Were there not ten cleansed? But where are the nine? Were there not any found who returned to give glory to God except this foreigner? " And He said to Him, "Arise, go your way. Your faith has made you well." (Luke 17:11-19)

TESTIMONIAL APPLICATION
The Struggle and Triumph of
Elder Lillian M. Hodges,
(as told by her daughter, Dr. Glenda F. Hodges)

She had been reasonably healthy even into her eighties. Most of her seldom complaints were usually attributed to her arthritis. However, sometime around her eighty-first birthday, she began to complain of shortness of breath and occasional lightheadedness. At this point, my brothers, sisters and I started to realize that she was having some respiratory discomfort. We immediately decided that we should take her to her primary care physician for a thorough examination. My mother had always styled herself as her "own" person and vowed to take care of herself for as long as she could.

Her first visit to her physician, Dr. Davis, after the onset of the symptoms I have described, indicated that further tests were needed. Mother agreed and she was referred to a cardiologist (a nice young boy as he was affectionately described by my mother because he appeared so youthful) who did a series of stress tests and cardiology type examinations. At the conclusion of his findings, he indicated that mother was beginning to show symptoms of congestive heart failure. He cautioned her to taper her activities and he prescribed several medications, including a diuretic.

As mother continued to celebrate birthday after birthday, around the age of eighty-four, she seemed to become very susceptible to colds. In November, 2005, mother contracted pneumonia and was hospitalized for 10 days. She was very, very ill but maintained to us that she was going to be alright. She constantly told us that God was not finished with her yet. She rebounded from the pneumonia, was discharged from the hospital and was able to be in her own home and bedroom for Christmas of 2005. During 2006, she seemed to be returning to her former self (before the CHF) diagnosis and was even able to take a few trips with me. However, in 2007, she contracted a second pneumonia and this time, she was even sicker than the first. Although she did not go to the hospital during this occurrence, she required constant monitoring. I spent two weeks with her and my eldest sister, a nurse, was with her almost constantly. Although my sister lived 100+ miles (round trip) away, she made mother her priority and ensured that her every need was met.

It was around August of 2007 when we begin to notice that mother was really declining. She was sicker than she wanted us to know. She became more congested, retained more fluids and generally had many days where she actually struggled to get out of bed and get dressed. Throughout her illness, mother maintained her faith in God and continued to go to church. She would often have long conversations with me (when her health permitted her to speak for long periods) and encouraged me to keep doing my best.

Mother drove herself to most of her outside activities. She drove to church, the grocery store, the hairdresser and almost any place else she felt she needed to go. Although we were all concerned about her health, we ultimately wanted her to maintain her sense of control. During the Christmas season of 2007, we all enjoyed a very memorable holiday with mother, all her children, her grandchildren and great grandchildren.

At the beginning of 2008, we all began to notice that mother was having seemingly more bad days than good; although, she would never complain. It seemed as if she coughed constantly and often had longer periods of shortness of breath. I vowed to spend as much time with her as I could because I felt that her days were getting shorter. As time continued, mother decided that she was readying herself for her transition. She began to make plans for her new residence. She packed up all of her shoes, had very interesting "end of life" conversations with me and toward the end of her life, she actually ceased to eat.

Three weeks before her passing, she drove herself to church and at the conclusion of the service; she told the pastor that he would not be seeing her again. On November 2, 2008 (Sunday) at 6:00 am, my mother passed away. Her struggles with CHF had been exchanged for the triumph of eternal life. Although there were many trips to the doctor and many medicines that were prescribed for her, my memories are more vivid of her never ending faith in God. She was ready to leave the world that she knew and start her life afresh in her heavenly home. Without a doubt, she fully embraced death. She truly epitomized Paul's discourse as he stated, to live is Christ but to die is gain! I am happy to know that my loss on earth was mother's gain in heaven.

Scriptural Support:

When the illness burden is magnified, requiring frequent hospitalizations, how does one maintain spiritual health?

The expert on this subject is the one whose journey has required facing numerous hospitalizations while maintaining a mental awareness of God's ability to heal. The following scripture offers an interesting perspective which we feel is worthy of consideration for anyone who has traveled this road.

> Therefore, I say to you, do not worry about your life, what you will eat or what you will drink; nor about your body, what you will put on...Therefore do not worry, saying, 'What shall we eat' or 'What shall we drink or 'what shall we wear,' for after these thing the Gentiles seek." For your heavenly Father knows that you need all these things. But seek ye first the kingdom of God and his righteousness, and all these things shall be added to you. Therefore do not worry about tomorrow, for tomorrow will worry about its own things. Sufficient for the day is its own trouble.
> (Matthew 6:25a, 31-34).

> Give us this day our daily bread. (Matthew 6:11)

Will God visit and deliver me in my affliction?

> You, who fear the Lord, praise Him!
> All you descendants of Jacob, glorify Him,
> And fear Him, all you offspring of Israel!
> For He has not despised nor abhorred the affliction of the afflicted;
> Nor has He hidden His face from Him;
> But when He cried to Him, He heard. (Psalm 22:23-24)

Turn yourself to me, and have mercy on me,
For I am desolate and afflicted.
The troubles of my heart have enlarged;
Bring me out of my distresses!
Look on my affliction and my pain,
And forgive all my sins. (Psalm 25:16-18).

Many are the afflictions of the righteous,
But the Lord delivers him out of them all. (Psalm 34:19)

Nevertheless He regarded their affliction,
When He heard their cry; (Psalm 106:44)

This is my comfort in my affliction,
For your word has given me life. (Psalm 119:50)

Hear my prayer, O Lord,
And let my cry come to You.
Do not hide your face from me in the day of my trouble;
Incline your ear to me;
In the day that I call, answer me speedily.
For my days are consumed like smoke,
And my bones are burned like a hearth.
My heart is stricken and withered like grass,
So that I forget to eat my bread... (Psalm 102:1-4)

When afflictions are brought on by my past behaviors; how can I change my future?

Teach me good judgment and knowledge,
For I believe Your commandments.

> Before I was afflicted I went astray,
> But now I keep Your word.
> You are good, and do good;
> Teach me your statutes. (Psalm 119:66-68)

> It is good for me that I have been afflicted,
> That I may learn your statutes. (Psalm 119:71)

> I am afflicted very much;
> Revive me, O Lord, according to Your word. (Psalm 119:107)

Will my visit with one who is afflicted make a difference?

> Is anyone among you suffering? Let him pray. Is anyone cheerful? Let him sing psalms. Is anyone among you sick? Let him call for the elders of the church, and let them pray over him, anointing him with oil in the name of the Lord. And the prayer of faith will save the sick and the Lord will raise him up. And if he has committed sins, he will be forgiven. Confess your trespasses to one another, and pray for one another, that you may be healed. The effective, fervent prayer of a righteous man avails much. (James 5:13-16)

TESTIMONIAL APPLICATION
Evangelist J's Delivery from Affliction
(as told by Dr. Betton)

Early one morning while on morning rounds I arrived at the bedside of a remarkable 75 year old woman, a self-described evangelist who always attended her denominations' quarterly conferences in Atlanta, Georgia, Memphis, Tennessee and Detroit, Michigan. In fact, I would make sure that her office appointments never interfered with her meeting schedules and would tease her if she failed to attend. Evangelist J, the name I will use in this narrative, was admitted with chest pain and had completed a selective coronary angiogram. When I arrived she told me the cardiologist's conclusion; she had inoperable disease and nothing could be done. She told me that the cardiologist told her that the only thing to offer was medication.

I listened to her as I held her hand and told her that I knew exactly the consultation necessary to overcome this problem. I opened my black physician's rounding bag, pulled out my portable Bible and shared scripture with her. I followed this with a prayer, in the name of Jesus, that he intervene in her coronary artery situation and make a difference in the life of this person who loved Him so much.

Evangelist J lived an additional 20 years before her death from a dementia related illness at the age of 95. Several years before her death, she had a repeat coronary angiogram that demonstrated new blood vessels around the previously blocked ones. Essentially, Evangelist J received a divine coronary artery bypass that rendered her free of chest pain for the remainder of her life.

Evangelist J is with the Lord and is unable to share this testimony but as her family physician of 20 years, this is but one of several testimonies from my archives of experiences that is appropriate for this subject.

Scriptures that Enhance Coping Skills:

When placed in a short or long term care facility how can I spiritually cope? How can others help me when my sanity becomes challenged through illness or loneliness?

Nearly every short or long term care facility that we have ever visited has spiritual care and/or support. Neighboring churches hold meetings, sing-a-longs and sometimes even worship services. Those in attendance enjoy it and attend frequently; however, there are always those persons, who by virtue of their medical conditions, are unable to attend. These persons are often viewed as the lost or un-churched, in the midst of a sea of persons. We have included this section with those persons in mind. This information is applicable to anyone receiving medical care in these institutional settings.

When the visit's charm has ended, the love one has been fed and all is fairly well, how do I turn the conversation to spiritual coping?

A. Prayer
   Heal me, O Lord, and I shall be healed;
   Save me, and I shall be saved,
   For You are my praise.

   Indeed they say to me,
   "Where is the word of the Lord?
   Let it come now!" (Jeremiah 17:14-15)

   O Lord, my strength and my fortress,

My refuge in the day of affliction, (Jeremiah 16:19a)

I have been young, and now am old;
Yet I have not seen the righteous forsaken,
Nor his descendants begging bread. (Psalm 37:25)

I will bless the Lord at all times;
His praise shall continually be in my mouth.
My soul shall make its boast in the Lord;
The humble shall hear of it and be glad.
Oh, magnify the Lord with me,
And let us exalt His name together. (Psalm 34:1-3)

I know, O Lord, that Your judgments are right,
And that in faithfulness you have afflicted me.
Yet I pray that your merciful kindness be my comfort,
According to Your word to your servant.
Let Your tender mercies come to me, that I may live.
(Psalm 119:75-77)

B. Assurance

The eyes of the Lord are on the righteous,
And his ears are open to their cry. (Psalm 34:15)

This is my comfort in my affliction,
For Your word has given me life. (Psalm 119:50)

And it shall come to pass that before they call, I will answer;
And while they are still speaking, I will hear. (Isaiah 65:24)

For thus says the Lord:

"Behold, I will extend peace to her like a river,

And the glory of the Gentiles like a flowing stream."

Then you shall feed;

On her sides shall you be carried,

And be dandled on her knees.

As one whom his mother comforts,

So I will comfort you;

And you shall be comforted in Jerusalem."

(Isaiah 66:12-13)

Call to me, and I will answer you, and show you great and mighty things, which you do not know. (Jeremiah 33:3)

Ministering to the Terminally Ill

Perhaps one of the harder types of visits is to a loved one that is terminally ill. Contrary to what many may speculate, it is usually the case that those who are nearing death fully know and recognize the same. Many have verbalized a readiness for the transition. In these instances, it is often the visitor who needs to be prepared. This section is as much for the visitor as for the one facing transition into the arms of Jesus Christ. The following scriptures are presented for both meditation and sharing with the family of the one who is soon-to-be transitioned.

I have fought a good fight, I have finished the race, I have kept the faith. Finally, there is laid up for me the crown of righteousness, which the Lord, the righteous judge, will give to me on that Day, and not to me only but also to all who have loved His appearing.

(2 Timothy 4:7-8)

The days of our lives are seventy years;
And if by reason of strength they are eighty years,
Yet their boast is only labor and sorrow;
For it is soon cut off, and we fly away.

So teach us to number our days,
That we may gain a heart of wisdom.

Oh, satisfy us early with Your mercy,
That we may rejoice and be glad all our days!

Make us glad according to the days in which You have afflicted us, (Psalm 90: 10, 12, 14-15a)

Precious in the sight of the Lord is the death of His saints. (Psalm 116:15)

Let not your heart be troubled; you believe in God, believe also in Me. In my Father's house are many mansions; if it were not so, I would have told you. I go to prepare a place for you. And if I go and prepare a place for you, I will come again and receive you to myself; that where I am, there you may be also. And where I go you know, and the way you know." (John 14:1-3)

Then the King will say to those on His right hand, 'Come, you blessed of My Father, inherit the kingdom prepared for you from the foundation of the world: (Matthew 25:34)

I do not pray for these alone, but also for those who will

believe in Me through their word; that they all may be one, as You, Father, are in Me, and I in You; that they also may be one in Us, that the world may believe that You sent Me. And the glory which You gave me I have given them, that they may be one just as We are one. I in them, and You in Me; that they may be made perfect in one and that the world may know that You have sent Me and have loved them as You have loved Me. Father, I desire that they also whom You gave Me may be with Me where I am, that they may behold My glory which You have given Me; for You loved Me before the foundation of the world. (John 17:20-24)

Now this I say, brethren, that flesh and blood cannot inherit the kingdom of God; nor does corruption inherit incorruption. Behold I tell you a mystery: We shall not all sleep, but we shall be changed – In a moment, in the twinkling of an eye, at the last trumpet. For the trumpet will sound, and the dead will be raised incorruptible and we shall be changed. For this corruptible must put on incorruption and this mortal must put on immortality. So when this corruptible has put on incorruption, and this mortal has put on immortality, then shall be brought to pass the saying that is written: *"Death is swallowed up in victory."*

Therefore, my beloved brethren, be steadfast, immovable, always abounding in the work of the Lord, knowing that your labor is not in vain in the Lord. (I Corinthians 15:50-54, 58)

For the Lord Himself will descend from heaven with a shout, with the voice of an archangel, and with the trumpet of God.

And the dead in Christ will rise first. Then we who are alive and remain shall be caught up together with them in the clouds to meet the Lord in the air. And thus we shall always be with the Lord. Therefore comfort one another with these words.

(1 Thessalonians 4:16-18)

Then the dust will return to the earth as it was,
And the spirit will return to God who gave it.
(Ecclesiastes 12:7)

Blessed are those who do His commandments that they may have the right to the tree of life, and may enter through the gates into the city. (Revelation 22:14)

"I, Jesus, have sent My angel to testify to you these things in the churches. I am the root and the offspring of David, the bright and morning star." And the Spirit and the bride say, "Come!" And let him who hears say, "Come!" And let him who thirsts come. Whoever desires, let him take the water of life freely. (Revelation 22:16-17)

TESTIMONIAL APPLICATION
My Mother's Transition
(as told by her son, Dr. Harold B. Betton)

I am the sixth of seven children born to my parents. My mother was diagnosed with Alzheimer's dementia after my elder brother died of cancer in 1986. During the initial onset of her illness, my father was not sure what was occurring and shared those concerns with me. I had her examined and ultimately cared for by a dear fellow physician friend, from the beginning of her illness until the time of her death. Initially, my interactions with her were purely son to mother and this continued until late in her disease state when she became bedridden. In the mid 1980s, very little was known about this new named dementia and there was no medication for it. Mother taught home economics in the public school system for 35 years before retirement and prided herself on her appearance, the beauty of her home environment and most certainly her cooking.

Dad progressively assumed these duties and instead of our weekly dinner at my parent's home on Sunday, we began to go out for dinner every Sunday. I did not give that much thought, though my wife picked up on the fact that my mom was "not herself." The natural course of the disease certainly took its toll on her and when she became bedridden and knew no one, my relationship with her moved to a higher level. We basically became Christian brother communicating with Christian sister.

My visits with mom, each day after work, were filled with Bible reading and prayer. The Lord led me to realize that my visits were just as much for me as for her. You see, there is no way to minister to another without ministering to yourself! I noticed that whenever I read the Bible, she would become very calm and listen; the same would occur when I would hold her hand and pray. These visits remained the same until her death in 1989.

The week before her death, I was in Nassau, Bahamas on vacation with my wife and two young children. All that week, the Lord directed me to read the books of Genesis and Exodus. Strangely, the only words that kept repeating themselves to me were "she was born and later died." This thought bathed my mind all week.

Upon arriving home, as I customarily have always done, I called my dad and told him that we arrived home safely. He replied, "Son your mother died yesterday." Although I was shocked and saddened, I have to confess that since receiving that news, even twenty-one years later, I have yet to shed the first tear of grief! Just as I ministered to her during the final stage of her illness, I was ministering to myself. The Lord prepared me for his ultimate will, which was to call my mother to her heavenly home. I will always rejoice that He used me in her preparation process!

CHAPTER FOUR

The Fallacy of Spiritualizing Illness

What is Spiritual Healing?

One might think that it is inappropriate to consider the subject of spiritualizing illness. For purposes of this manual, we offer the following definition. Spiritualizing illness occurs when one places blame for the cause of an illness on some type of religious ground or claim healing on the basis of those grounds. In such instances, the ultimate result can lead to willful medical neglect in the face of clear evidence of the illness' presence or its progression. In order to elucidate this concept, we offer the following case study.

THE STORY OF AB

AB suffered from hypertension for many years and despite much urging for compliance with the assistance of medication and a solid dietary regimen, difficulties in managing the illness persisted. Her blood pressure readings remained out of control. After two or three hospitalizations, she showed some progress; however, once discharged, she resumed her bad dietary and non-compliance habits. Since she had a family history of renal failure, she was appropriately warned of this eventual possibility and her kidney functions were continually monitored. Despite best efforts, she developed abnormal kidney laboratory indices and was referred to a kidney specialist. Although dialysis was advised; she refused.

On a Monday morning visit to Dr. Betton's office, the patient confided in him that the previous day, the patient's pastor had prayed for her, anointed her with oil and pronounced her "healed." She proclaimed to Dr. Betton that she was no longer "claiming hypertension or kidney failure" and that she intended to cease taking all of her medications. Rather than becoming upset with the patient, Dr. Betton proposed that they test her proclamation of healing. He agreed to check her blood pressure and kidney functions that day and if her proclamation of healing was accurate, there would be no trace of either illness. The patient agreed. After tests were performed, it was discovered that both the blood pressure and kidney function measurements were consistent with those in the past. Neither condition was healed. Additionally, Dr. Betton explained to her the difference between claiming healing as a result of an emotional feeling and a divine pronouncement. He shared New Testament scripture with her in an effort to demonstrate that where instances of healing had occurred in the scriptures, the person had no lingering evidence of the illness.

In spite of the explanations offered to the patient and the indisputable proofs of scripture, AB refused to accept the information provided to her. She decided to hold fast to her belief that she was healed by prayer, the laying on of hands and the anointing with oil. Three months later, AB died from kidney failure and hypertension. Although Dr. Betton participated in her funeral, he remains regretful to this day, that AB decided to spiritualize medical reality.

We believe that an excellent starting point to enhance one's understanding of the spiritualizing of illness is to determine the genesis of the spiritualization. In AB's case, one must ask, "Did the

Pastor or the prayer service mislead her?" Other questions that come to mind are issues such as, "did she hear or derive what she wanted to hear," "did she want healing so badly that she was unable to hear," or was she simply so convinced that she would be healed that it did not matter what was told to her." Certainly, prayers outside of the will of God can mislead anyone. To that end, we believe that the crucial prayer in the face of an illness is that "God's will be done." Scripture supports the act of praying for healing. Consider the following:

Is there anyone among you suffering? Let him pray. Is anyone cheerful? Let him sing psalms. Is anyone among you sick? Let him call for the Elders of the church and let them pray over him, anointing him with oil in the name of the Lord. And the prayer of faith will save the sick and the Lord will raise him up. And if he has committed sins, he will be forgiven. Confess your trespasses to one another and pray for one another, that you may be healed. The effective, fervent prayer of a righteous man avails much. (James 5:13-16)

When anyone is praying for the sick, we suggest that the one who is praying plainly indicate in the context of the prayer service that they are praying that the will of God be done and that any healing that is manifested occur according to God's will. Further, it should be clearly indicated (if not in the prayer, then at some point) that healing does not occur by the hand of any human; however, God may use the human vessel as an agent of His will. When healing is defined and clarified in this manner, no one leaves the service mistaken about the outcome.

Scripture is replete with healing narratives and in each case where these narratives appear, the one who is healed manifests no evidence of the infirmity. There are instances where this healing occurs in prayer services and, in such cases, all are pleased and are able to rejoice. However, there are other times when healing is not as immediate and may not even manifest itself for several days, months or even years. Under these circumstances, one should remember that God heals in various ways. He sometimes uses physicians, lay people, nurses, other hospital personnel, clergy and even other believers to manifest His will and entire medical establishments to pronounce the same.

TESTIMONAL APPLICATION
The Story of L.T.

We offer the following story as an indication of a situation where the prayers of the righteous availed much. LT is a 30 year old, very well liked, African American young man whose family is well known in the community of Little Rock, Arkansas. In the dark hours of a Monday night while riding his motorcycle, he had an unfortunate accident and was ejected from the motorcyle. LT suffered a head injury and bleeding into the area of his brain. Dr. Betton received a phone call from a church member at 7:00 am because she received a phone call from the hospital informing her that LT was on life support and barely clinging to life. Extremely upset and shaken, she telephoned Dr. Betton, her pastor, and asked if he could leave the office and go to the hospital for family support. At that time, Dr. Betton was not able to leave; however, a former associate pastor, was able to respond.

Later during the same day, Dr. Betton visited the family and continued to do so each day during the first week of LT's hospitalization. The physicians caring for LT were well known to Dr. Betton and provided excellent medical and surgical care to LT. Although everyone was understandably upset about LT's accident, young people came from everywhere to visit him, support the family and to offer assistance in any way they could.

The community of faith at LT's church, the church where Dr. Betton pastors, and other churches in Memphis, Tennessee, were called on to pray specifically for LT. LT made daily progress and was ultimately discharged from the acute care area of the hospital into rehabilitation. At the writing of this manuscript, the greatest challenge that LT is experiencing is "staying in bed." He is determined to advance his rehabilitation schedule so that he can be discharged. The fractures that LT suffered during the accident were limited to his skull and face. In this experience, LT's accident and subsequent medical problems were purposefully presented to the community of faith and a call for healing and restoration was issued. The caveat, throughout all of the praying and beseeching the Lord, was the understanding that God's will for LT would be done and that those who prayed for him would likewise be able to accept the same.

While LT's situation may not necessarily be that unique, we offer it as an indication of how God moves in the face of illness. We further believe that it clearly distinguishes praying according to the will of God and spiritualizing a medical situation to the extent that claims and pronouncements are made that are inconsistent with God's will.

As we continue to dissect the notion of spiritualizing illness, we are convinced that much of the confusion surrounding this topic occurs as a result of persons attributing power to others to "heal," when in fact, that power belongs only to God. When God is removed as the object of divine intervention and is replaced by anyone else, the likelihood increases that the illness may become spiritualized and the patient may begin to seek those (humans) who are known to be "able to lay hands on the sick and they shall be healed." To guard against falling prey to such overwhelming individuals, it is important for the physician, clergy person laity or whomever it is who is petitioning God for healing, to clearly ask that God's will be done in the situation of the one who is ill. When discussion or prayer is made in this way, there can be no confusion about the prayer, its intent or God's role in the process of praying.

Suggested Scriptures:

We offer these scriptures and explanations in an effort to clarify the concept of healing and we commend these scriptures to you for your reading and meditation.

John 5:1-14 - Jesus heals the man at the pool at Bethsaida

[1] After this there was a feast of the Jews; and Jesus went up to Jerusalem.

[2] Now there is at Jerusalem by the sheep market a pool, which is called in the Hebrew tongue Bethesda, having five porches.

[3] In these lay a great multitude of impotent folk, of blind, halt, withered, waiting for the moving of the water.

[4] For an angel went down at a certain season into the pool, and troubled the water: whosoever then first after the troubling of the water stepped in was made whole of whatsoever disease he had.

[5] And a certain man was there, which had an infirmity thirty and eight years.

[6] When Jesus saw him lie, and knew that he had been now a long time in that case, he saith unto him, Wilt thou be made whole?

[7] The impotent man answered him, Sir, I have no man, when the water is troubled, to put me into the pool: but while I am coming, another steppeth down before me.

[8] Jesus saith unto him, Rise, take up thy bed, and walk.

[9] And immediately the man was made whole, and took up his bed, and walked: and on the same day was the sabbath.

[10] The Jews therefore said unto him that was cured, It is the sabbath day: it is not lawful for thee to carry thy bed.

[11] He answered them, He that made me whole, the same said unto me, Take up thy bed, and walk.

[12] Then asked they him, What man is that which said unto thee, Take up thy bed, and walk?

[13] And he that was healed wist not who it was: for Jesus had conveyed himself away, a multitude being in that place.

[14] Afterward Jesus findeth him in the temple, and said unto him, Behold, thou art made whole: sin no more, lest a worse thing come unto thee.

The important implication of this passage is Jesus' question and the man's response. The man was asked whether he wanted to be made whole (complete restoration mentally, physically and spiritually). He answered in the affirmative. The difference between being the first in the pool and Jesus' healing was the extent of that healing. As indicated by the scripture, the first person in the pool was merely healed of his/her infirmity; he/she was not made whole. When we invite God into the healing process, it is important to recognize that God has no limits.

Matthew 17:14-21 -- the difficult healing

Another challenge associated with prayer and healing occurs when there is no obvious change in the person as detected by the one who is praying. In such a situation, what is the appriopriate response? The best description of this dilemma is illustrated by Jesus in Matthew 17:14-21. This passage of scripture outlines Jesus' healing an epileptic boy. Jesus' conclusion is found in the last verse. He does not imply that the child could not be healed; he noted that some persons do not manifest healing at the time of prayer.

[14] And when they were come to the multitude, there came to him a certain man, kneeling down to him, and saying,

[15] Lord, have mercy on my son: for he is lunatick, and sore vexed: for ofttimes he falleth into the fire and oft into the water.

[16] And I brought him to thy disciples and they could not cure him.

[17] Then Jesus answered and said, O faithless and perverse generation, how long shall I be with you? how long shall I suffer you? bring him hither to me.

[18] And Jesus rebuked the devil; and he departed out of him: and the child was cured from that very hour.

[19] Then came the disciples to Jesus apart, and said, Why could not we cast him out?

[20] And Jesus said unto them, Because of your unbelief: for verily I say unto you, If ye have faith as a grain of mustard seed, ye shall say unto this mountain, Remove hence to yonder place; and it shall remove; and nothing shall be impossible unto you.

[21] Howbeit this kind goeth not out but by prayer and fasting.

Matthew 9:2-7 Illness because of sin

Another dimension of illness requiring prayer occurs when the illness appears to be connected with disobedience to God or unrighteousness behavior. There are many persons that are sick or are suffering from the effects of lingering illnesses because of sin in their lives. Jesus plainly indicates that these persons must first be forgiven of their sins and secondarily healed, if that healing is within the will of God.

Consider Matthew 9:2-7.

[2] And, behold, they brought to him a man sick of the palsy,

lying on a bed: and Jesus seeing their faith said unto the sick of the palsy; Son, be of good cheer; thy sins be forgiven thee.

[3] And, behold, certain of the scribes said within themselves, This man blasphemeth.

[4] And Jesus knowing their thoughts said, Wherefore think ye evil in your hearts?

[5] For whether is easier, to say, Thy sins be forgiven thee; or to say, Arise, and walk?

[6] But that ye may know that the Son of man hath power on earth to forgive sins, (then saith he to the sick of the palsy,) Arise, take up thy bed, and go unto thine house.

[7] And he arose, and departed to his house.

Luke 8:43-48 The faith that heals

There are times when one comes to the Lord on his/her personal behalf, seeking restoration. These are not necessarily times when they seek others to pray for them; but rather, they seek a private audience with the Chief Physician, much like the woman in this story. The great caveat of this story is the woman's definite knowledge that healing did, in fact, occur as a result of the change in her symptoms. Consider the details of this story.

[43] And a woman having an issue of blood twelve years, which had spent all her living upon physicians, neither could be healed of any,

[44] Came behind him, and touched the border of his garment: and immediately her issue of blood stanched.

[45] And Jesus said, Who touched me? When all denied, Peter and they that were with him said, Master, the multitude throng thee and press thee, and sayest thou, Who touched me?

[46] And Jesus said, Somebody hath touched me: for I perceive that virtue is gone out of me.

[47] And when the woman saw that she was not hid, she came trembling, and falling down before him, she declared unto him before all the people for what cause she had touched him and how she was healed immediately.

[48] And he said unto her, Daughter, be of good comfort: thy faith hath made thee whole; go in peace.

Unsolicited healing as a result of faithful service -- Luke 13:11-13

Luke records the story of a woman who most likely suffered from osteoporosis with vertebral involvement, causing her to slump over. Many of us have seen older women and men who similarly slump and seem incapable of standing erect. There are two points to this story. First of all, the woman did not allow her condition to prevent her from worship and secondly, Jesus used her experience to demonstrate an example of the power of praise. Consider this story.

> [11] And, behold, there was a woman which had a spirit of infirmity eighteen years, and was bowed together, and could in no wise lift up herself.
>
> [12] And when Jesus saw her, he called her to him, and said unto her, Woman, thou art loosed from thine infirmity.
>
> [13] And he laid his hands on her: and immediately she was made straight, and glorified God.

Many examples of healings, such as the ones illustrated here, can be gleaned from scripture. The underlying tone of each is the will of God in the healing, as well as the pronouncement by Him that all is well. As mere men and women, we must be careful when permitting others to attribute to us the capacity to heal. We must always remember that if God does not heal, healing does not occur. God may intend for a cure, or certain amelioration of the condition to occur in some way that is not associated or even connected with the one who is praying at the time or the praying event. We recommend that one always pray that God's will is manifested in the life of the one seeking prayer. Accordingly, the next chapter is devoted entirely to this subject.

CHAPTER FIVE

Praying According to the Will of God

How is one to determine the will of God?

Rather than attempt to teach prayer as a specific subject, we offer this material to highlight the simple fact that we can only pray according to God's will. Often we do not know His will and are left with the responsibility of praying that His will be manifest in the life or lives of His children. There are many scriptural references supporting this assertion. Answers to questions presented drive this chapter's content and presentation.

What must the one praying know about prayer?

Mark 11:23-24 The one praying must do so with resolute faith.

> [23] For verily I say unto you, That whosoever shall say unto this mountain, Be thou removed, and be thou cast into the sea; and shall not doubt in his heart, but shall believe that those things which he saith shall come to pass; he shall have whatsoever he saith.
>
> [24] Therefore I say unto you, What things soever ye desire, when ye pray, believe that ye receive them, and ye shall have them.

1 John 5:14-15 Prayer requires confidence.

> [14] And this is the confidence that we have in him, that, if we ask any thing according to his will, he heareth us:
>
> [15] And if we know that he hears us, whatsoever we ask, we know that we have the petitions that we desired of him.

Hebrew 4:16 Prayer requires approaching God with the correct attitude.

> [16] Let us therefore come boldly unto the throne of grace, that we may obtain mercy, and find grace to help in time of need.

1 John 2:15-16 Prayer requires the one praying to have the motive of glorifying God.

> [15] Love not the world, neither the things that are in the world. If any man love the world, the love of the Father is not in him.
>
> [16] For all that is in the world, the lust of the flesh, and the lust of the eyes, and the pride of life, is not of the Father, but is of the world.

John 14:13-14 Prayer requires one to pray in the Name of Jesus Christ.

> [13] And whatsoever ye shall ask in my name, that will I do, that the Father may be glorified in the Son.
>
> [14] If ye shall ask any thing in my name, I will do it.

Is knowing God's will easily attainable?

This is perhaps the hardest of the questions presented because it requires that one recognizes God's intention. As such, it is important for the one praying to realize some inescapable truths. Consider the following.

It is God's will that His children live eternally with Him.

[1] Let not your heart be troubled: ye believe in God, believe also in me.

[2] In my Father's house are many mansions: if it were not so, I would have told you. I go to prepare a place for you.

[3] And if I go and prepare a place for you, I will come again, and receive you unto myself; that where I am, there ye may be also.

[4] And whither I go ye know, and the way ye know. (John 14:1-4)

[51] Verily, verily, I say unto you, If a man keep my saying, he shall never see death. (John 8:51)

It is God's will that all men come to know Him?

[29] For whom he did foreknow, he also did predestinate to be conformed to the image of his Son, that he might be the firstborn among many brethren.

[30] Moreover whom he did predestinate, them he also called: and whom he called, them he also justified: and whom he justified, them he also glorified. (Romans 8:29-30)

[14] But whosoever drinketh of the water that I shall give him shall never thirst; but the water that I shall give him shall be in him a well of water springing up into everlasting life. (John 4:14)

It is God's will that His children be obedient.

Then said Jesus to those Jews which believed on him, If ye continue in my word, then are ye my disciples indeed. (John 8:31)

It is God's will that we not lose heart in tribulation.

> [22] And ye now therefore have sorrow: but I will see you again, and your heart shall rejoice, and your joy no man taketh from you.
>
> [23] And in that day ye shall ask me nothing. Verily, verily, I say unto you, Whatsoever ye shall ask the Father in my name, he will give it you.
>
> [33] These things I have spoken unto you, that in me ye might have peace. In the world ye shall have tribulation: but be of good cheer; I have overcome the world. (John 16: 22, 23, 33)

It is God's will that we be kept from the power of Satan (John 17:15-16) and as such, be separated unto him by His Word. (John 17:17)

> [15] I pray not that thou shouldest take them out of the world, but that thou shouldest keep them from the evil.
>
> [16] They are not of the world, even as I am not of the world.
>
> [17] Sanctify them through thy truth: thy word is truth.
>
> It is God's will that we be not condemned under the Law.
>
> [14] Blotting out the handwriting of ordinances that were against us, which was contrary to us, and took it out of the way, nailing it to his cross. (Colossians 2:14)

It is God's will that we stay away from fleshly entangle-ments.

> [1] Stand fast therefore in the liberty wherewith Christ hath made us free, and be not entangled again with the yoke of bondage. (Galatians 5:1)
>
> [3] Thou wilt keep him in perfect peace, whose mind is stayed on thee: because he trusteth in thee. (Isaiah 26:3)

The recognition of these truths should guide the one praying in his or her quest to understand God's will even though scripture sustains the fact that all prayers require intercessory intervention by the Holy Spirit.

Likewise the Spirit also helps in our weaknesses. For we do not know what we should pray for as we ought, but the Spirit Himself makes intercession for us with groanings which cannot be uttered. (Romans 8:26)

Can one pray in the will of God and be specific in the prayer petition?

Prayer is communication with God. In reality, it represents a speech act. Prayers manifest requests to God and the one who is praying accepts the response by faith. The following passages of Scripture invite us to the table of petition, even though some of the passages fail to identify the one who is praying.

The Lord responded to the outcries against Sodom and Gomorrah.

> And the Lord said, "Because the outcry against Sodom and Gomorrah is great, and because their sin is very great, I will go down now and see whether they have done altogether according to the outcry against it that has come to Me; and if not, I will know." (Genesis 18:20-21)

The Lord responded to the outcries of the enslaved Israelites in Egypt.

> And the Lord said: "I have surely seen the oppression of My people who are in Egypt, and have heard their cry because of their taskmasters, for I know their sorrows. So I have come down to deliver them out of the hand of the Egyptians, and to bring them up from that land to a good and large land, to a land flowing with milk and honey, to the place of the Canaanites and the Hittites and the Amorites and the Perizzites and the Hivites and the Jebusites. Now behold the cry of the children of Israel has come to Me, and I have also

seen the oppression with which the Egyptians oppress them. (Exodus 3:7-9)

Hannah prayed that God would grant her prayer to conceive a son.

[8] Then said Elkanah her husband to her, Hannah, why weepest thou? and why eatest thou not? and why is thy heart grieved? am not I better to thee than ten sons?

[9] So Hannah rose up after they had eaten in Shiloh, and after they had drunk. Now Eli the priest sat upon a seat by a post of the temple of the LORD.

[10] And she was in bitterness of soul, and prayed unto the LORD, and wept sore.

[11] And she vowed a vow, and said, O LORD of hosts, if thou wilt indeed look on the affliction of thine handmaid, and remember me, and not forget thine handmaid, but wilt give unto thine handmaid a man child, then I will give him unto the LORD all the days of his life, and there shall no razor come upon his head.

[19] And they rose up in the morning early, and worshipped before the LORD, and returned, and came to their house to Ramah: and Elkanah knew Hannah his wife; and the LORD remembered her.

[20] Wherefore it came to pass, when the time was come about after Hannah had conceived, that she bare a son, and called his name Samuel, saying, Because I have asked him of the LORD. (1 Samuel 1:8-11, 19-20)

Did Jesus pray that we have access to God and receive His grace?

Jesus provided an outline for the model prayer. An exacting study of its contents provide a good framework for understanding prayer.

[5] And when thou prayest, thou shalt not be as the hypocrites are: for they love to pray standing in the synagogues and in the corners of the streets, that they may be seen of men. Verily I say unto you, They have their reward.

[6] But thou, when thou prayest, enter into thy closet, and when thou hast shut thy door, pray to thy Father which is in secret; and thy Father which seeth in secret shall reward thee openly.

[7] But when ye pray, use not vain repetitions, as the heathen do: for they think that they shall be heard for their much speaking.

[8] Be not ye therefore like unto them: for your Father knoweth what things ye have need of, before ye ask him.

[9] After this manner therefore pray ye: Our Father which art in heaven, Hallowed be thy name.

[10] Thy kingdom come. Thy will be done in earth, as it is in heaven.

[11] Give us this day our daily bread.

[12] And forgive us our debts, as we forgive our debtors.

[13] And lead us not into temptation, but deliver us from evil: For thine is the kingdom, and the power, and the glory, for ever. Amen. (Matthew 6:5-13)

It is the Lord's desire that all believers live with Him eternally. He desires that we live life more abundantly as we abide in His word. Consider the medley of relevant scriptures that follow.

4] Abide in me, and I in you. As the branch cannot bear fruit of itself, except it abide in the vine; no more can ye, except ye abide in me.

[5] I am the vine, ye are the branches: He that abideth in me,

and I in him, the same bringeth forth much fruit: for without me ye can do nothing.

[6] If a man abide not in me, he is cast forth as a branch, and is withered; and men gather them, and cast them into the fire, and they are burned.

[7] If ye abide in me, and my words abide in you, ye shall ask what ye will, and it shall be done unto you.

[8] Herein is my Father glorified, that ye bear much fruit; so shall ye be my disciples. (John 15:4-8)

[20] Neither pray I for these alone, but for them also which shall believe on me through their word;

[21] That they all may be one; as thou, Father, art in me, and I in thee, that they also may be one in us: that the world may believe that thou hast sent me.

[22] And the glory which thou gavest me I have given them; that they may be one, even as we are one:

[23] I in them, and thou in me, that they may be made perfect in one; and that the world may know that thou hast sent me, and hast loved them, as thou hast loved me.

[24] Father, I will that they also, whom thou hast given me, be with me where I am; that they may behold my glory, which thou hast given me: for thou lovedst me before the foundation of the world.

[25] O righteous Father, the world hath not known thee: but I have known thee, and these have known that thou hast sent me.

[26] And I have declared unto them thy name, and will declare it: that the love wherewith thou hast loved me may be in them, and I in them. (John 17:20-26)

[10] The thief cometh not, but for to steal, and to kill, and to destroy: I am come that they might have life, and that they might have it more abundantly. (John 10:10)

When we are stressed or seriously bothered, can we take anything to God in prayer?

To pray that one is relieved of conditions of stress is your right, as a child of God. The most awe inspiring references is represented by King Hezekiah, an 8th century Judean King during the time of the Assyrian insurgency. Consider two scriptural passages; the first as a response to Assyrian ambassadors wishing to render Judea as a vassal state and the second, in response to a terminal illness afflicting Hezekiah. The following passages elucidate the threat of Assyria to the people, Hezekiah's prayer and God's response.

[1] Now it came to pass in the fourteenth year of king Hezekiah, that Sennacherib king of Assyria came up against all the defenced cities of Judah, and took them.

[2] And the king of Assyria sent Rabshakeh from Lachish to Jerusalem unto King Hezekiah with a great army. And he stood by the conduit of the upper pool in the highway of the fuller's field.

[3] Then came forth unto him Eliakim, Hilkiah's son, which was over the house, and Shebna the scribe, and Joah, Asaph's son, the recorder.

[4] And Rabshakeh said unto them, Say ye now to Hezekiah, Thus saith the great king, the king of Assyria, What confidence is this wherein thou trustest?

[5] I say, sayest thou, (but they are but vain words) I have counsel and strength for war: now on whom dost thou trust, that thou rebellest against me?

[6] Lo, thou trustest in the staff of this broken reed, on Egypt;

whereon if a man lean, it will go into his hand, and pierce it: so is Pharaoh king of Egypt to all that trust in him.

[7] But if thou say to me, We trust in the LORD our God: is it not he, whose high places and whose altars Hezekiah hath taken away, and said to Judah and to Jerusalem, Ye shall worship before this altar?

[8] Now therefore give pledges, I pray thee, to my master the king of Assyria and I will give thee two thousand horses, if thou be able on thy part to set riders upon them.

(Isaiah 36:1-8)

[14] And Hezekiah received the letter from the hand of the messengers, and read it: and Hezekiah went up unto the house of the LORD, and spread it before the LORD.

[15] And Hezekiah prayed unto the LORD, saying,

[16] O LORD of hosts, God of Israel, that dwellest between the cherubims, thou art the God, even thou alone, of all the kingdoms of the earth: thou hast made heaven and earth.

[17] Incline thine ear, O LORD, and hear; open thine eyes, O LORD, and see: and hear all the words of Sennacherib, which hath sent to reproach the living God.

[18] Of a truth, LORD, the kings of Assyria have laid waste all the nations, and their countries,

[19] And have cast their gods into the fire: for they were no gods, but the work of men's hands, wood and stone: therefore they have destroyed them.

[20] Now therefore, O LORD our God, save us from his hand, that all the kingdoms of the earth may know that thou art the LORD, even thou only.

[21] Then Isaiah the son of Amoz sent unto Hezekiah, saying,

Thus saith the LORD God of Israel, Whereas thou hast prayed to me against Sennacherib king of Assyria:

[22] This is the word which the LORD hath spoken concerning him; The virgin, the daughter of Zion, hath despised thee, and laughed thee to scorn; the daughter of Jerusalem hath shaken her head at thee.

[23] Whom hast thou reproached and blasphemed? and against whom hast thou exalted thy voice, and lifted up thine eyes on high? even against the Holy One of Israel.

[24] By thy servants hast thou reproached the Lord, and hast said, By the multitude of my chariots am I come up to the height of the mountains, to the sides of Lebanon; and I will cut down the tall cedars thereof, and the choice fir trees thereof: and I will enter into the height of his border, and the forest of his Carmel.

[25] I have digged, and drunk water; and with the sole of my feet have I dried up all the rivers of the besieged places.

[26] Hast thou not heard long ago, how I have done it; and of ancient times, that I have formed it? now have I brought it to pass, that thou shouldest be to lay waste defenced cities into ruinous heaps.

[27] Therefore their inhabitants were of small power, they were dismayed and confounded: they were as the grass of the field, and as the green herb, as the grass on the housetops, and as corn blasted before it be grown up.

[28] But I know thy abode, and thy going out, and thy coming in, and thy rage against me.

[29] Because thy rage against me, and thy tumult, is come up into mine ears, therefore will I put my hook in thy nose, and

my bridle in thy lips, and I will turn thee back by the way by which thou camest.

[30] And this shall be a sign unto thee, Ye shall eat this year such as groweth of itself; and the second year that which springeth of the same: and in the third year sow ye, and reap, and plant vineyards, and eat the fruit thereof.

[31] And the remnant that is escaped of the house of Judah shall again take root downward, and bear fruit upward:

[32] For out of Jerusalem shall go forth a remnant, and they that escape out of mount Zion: the zeal of the LORD of hosts shall do this.

[33] Therefore thus saith the LORD concerning the king of Assyria, He shall not come into this city, nor shoot an arrow there nor come before it with shields, nor cast a bank against it. (Isaiah 37: 14-33)

Hezekiah's plight, petition and pronouncement.

[1] In those days was Hezekiah sick unto death. And Isaiah the prophet the son of Amoz came unto him, and said unto him, Thus saith the LORD, Set thine house in order: for thou shalt die, and not live.

[2] Then Hezekiah turned his face toward the wall, and prayed unto the LORD,

[3] And said, Remember now, O LORD, I beseech thee, how I have walked before thee in truth and with a perfect heart, and have done that which is good in thy sight. And Hezekiah wept sore.

[4] Then came the word of the LORD to Isaiah, saying,

[5] Go, and say to Hezekiah, Thus saith the LORD, the God of David thy father, I have heard thy prayer, I have seen thy tears: behold, I will add unto thy days fifteen years. (Isaiah 38:1-5)

TESTIMONIAL APPLICATION
A Son's Prayer and His Father's Transition
Dr. Harold B. Betton

My father was a true man of God, retiree of the Agricultural Extension Service with 45 years of service, servant of many and child of God. As a father, he taught us everything from algebra to basic carpentry. Upon my return from medical training, my relationship with my father translated from boy and dad to professional and dad. I grew very close to him and I can truly say that he became my "best friend."

Dad had heart disease and diabetes and as time unfolded, the heart problems worsened. Either my wife or I would accompany him on his many office visits to his physician and we would always make sure that we understood everything in order for him (my dad) to follow the therapeutic instructions. This worked well for several years until the natural course of his illness worsened. Eventually dad's condition required that he be hospitalized.

A peculiar thing happened on the first day of his hospitalization. After getting him into his room, he asked me to close the door. As an obedient son, I most certainly complied with his every request. Dad then unfolded his verbal will to me. He said: "If I don't make it out of here I want you to do..." I looked him in the face, eye to eye and told him that I would follow his every wish. Dad knew that I would always obey him; he was partly the reason why I never failed at anything. I always wanted to please him.

Dad had a 5 vessel coronary artery bypass and an additional

surgery to fix a circulation problem in his leg. This went well; however, his intensive unit course was rocky at best. Seemingly every waking moment was spent in a state of prayer and many times daily I would drop to my knees and petition the Lord for his healing . Ironically, I ended all prayers with "nevertheless, not my will but yours, Lord, be done. I will accept it." I visited my dad regularly and talked with the nurses and his physicians on a daily basis. I had the additional responsibility of relating his condition to out-of-town family, maintaining my medical practice, being an effective husband and father, and pastoring a local congregation.

Dad developed an infection and had to return to surgery. This concerned us greatly. All the time my prayers remain consistent. "Lord, you said that we receive not because we ask not. I don't want to be remiss and not ask you for my father's healing; you know I want my dad well. Nevertheless, not my will Lord, but I will accept your will for him."

I received a STAT page that my dad's condition worsened. My wife and I raced to the hospital and when I peered in I will never forget what I saw. The surgeon, a friend of mine and his cardiologist, another friend, were conducting resusitative efforts on my dad. My father's chest was opened and I saw the cardiovascular surgeon's hand in my dad's chest cavity massaging his heart. I know that my wife did not see it because we had no subsequent conversation about it. Although I was not in the room, I was able to discern the sea of machines, IV poles and beds in the intensive care unit. I turned with my wife and walked into the quiet room to wait for the verdict. Yes, I was tearful; yes, my wife was tearful. Two hospital chaplains accompanied us and just sat. I do not recall them saying anything; however, I do recall that I was so pleased that they were silent. I had prayed so much, so often, so intensely that I felt I had the answer from

God. My dad had run his race, finished his course and received the healing for which I had been praying. He was with HIM. This taught me the true meaning of nevertheless, not my will, but God's will be done. I accepted God's will.

It has been 16 years since this incident and it is as fresh in my mind at this time as it was on that day. The lesson learned will be forever etched in my mind. I have never shared this in print before; however, I have shared the story with many people in an attempt to demonstrate that praying according to the will of God is primary for all of us.

CHAPTER SIX

Ministering to Family and Love Ones

Does ministering to family members ever present a challenge?

Ministering to family and love ones can sometimes become a very arduous task. This chapter is devoted to extinguishing the anxiety of the minister designee, clergy or physician-clergy who may be a member of the family unit. Ministering, in this context, does not imply anything pastoral; it represents that person within or outside the family unit that carries the responsibility of ministering to the family and love ones during the course of a family member's illness. Someone should be assigned the task of directing the family during these situations. Navigating the healthcare system may present as daunting or even frightening to many.

As a family physician, Dr. Betton's responsibility as navigator is only understood, or appreciated when demonstrated to those he serves. One might ask, "how is this best done or, when is it best done?" The following illustration will set the tone for our discussion in this chapter.

The Case Study of WC (as told by Dr. Betton)

WC died in 2009 from cancer of the lung. I had been her physician for over 20 years and cared for her, her daughters and grandchildren.

She never came to the office alone because one of her faithful daughters always accompanied her. She had controlled diabetes, hypertension and dyslipidemia (elevated cholesterol). Ms. WC was a nonsmoker and a nondrinker. On one of her visits, she presented with a history of a bad cough and cold. I examined her and X-rayed her chest. A mass was discoved on X-ray and I hospitalized her. She was diagnosed with lung cancer that could not be surgically handled. She was assigned chemotherapy. This frightened her children and the usually talkative WC remained very quiet.

I arranged an office meeting for the family and WC for the purpose of charting a course of action for her care. I opened the meeting with these words: "Thank you for coming today because WC has cancer of the lung and I do not know God's will for her life. We need to chart a course that covers any circumstance." I discussed the role of the oncologist (cancer specialist), pulmonologist (lung specialist) and the radiation therapist. I discussed the likelihood of frequent hospitalizations and I discussed advance directives, healthcare proxy and the need for (or against) resusitation.

Since I knew the family well and sensed that WC's remaining time on earth was probably short, I was very intentional about the need for one of her children to be able to make appropriate decisions on WC's behalf after necesary collaborations with other family members. Sometime after this family meeting, we all talked again and the children shared WC's wishes with me. WC was always present at each family meeting.

After the family decided that resusitation would not be an option, we discussed estate issues. I told WC that it was time for her to make sure that bank accounts and other instruments, insurance, etc. were known to her children and appropriately worded so there would not be any confusion, should it be God's will for her (WC) to be with Him.

WC was hospitalized that final time and died in the intensive care unit. To this day, I still take care of the daughters and grandchildren. They thanked me for helping them navigate the healthcare system and as a family, remain on one accord.

Ministry to Others is Always the Will of God.

In the Sermon on the Mount, Jesus asked a rhetorical question to illustrate a point about judging. "Can the blind lead the blind? Shall they not both fall into the ditch?"[10] Though Jesus asks this question in the context of judging, the truth translates to our subject. People need help! Someone has to take the reigns and support, navigate and reach out to lead the hurting. In this regard, Jesus has provided very clear direction. Consider the following:

> Blessed are they that mourn: for they shall be comforted. (Matt 5:3)

> Blessed are they which do hunger and thirst after righteousness: for they shall be filled. (Matt 5:6)

> Blessed are the merciful: for they shall obtain mercy. (Matt 5:7)

> Be careful for nothing; but in everything by prayer and supplication with thanksgiving let your requests be made known unto God. And the peace of God, with passeth all understanding, shall keep your hearts and minds through Christ Jesus. (Phil 4:6-7)

A closer look at Jesus' words in Matthew teaches us that we do mourn, thirst and/or need favor. People hurt and they are promised

---

10   Luke 6:39

divine comfort. This divine comfort is often provided by a human minister. That person may be a family member, friend, casual acquaintance, clergy person, or healthcare professional. A person whose life can be chronicled by service prays for divine intervention and favor, especially in times of hurt. Jesus promised this in Matthew 5:7.

We are not implying that Jesus needs any human help in this process; we merely state that sensivitiy to the needs of others allows us to be more effective ministers of God's word in our day by day work. People quote the prayer of Jabez[11] but fail to live it. As effective ministers of God, we are expected to minister to family and love ones.

Paul's letter to the Philippian church contained a prescription for anxiety (Phillipians 4:5-9) predicated upon their faith. Verse 9 provided a template for them and for us. "Those things, which ye have both learned, and received, and heard and seen in me, do. And the God of peace shall be with you." With this statement, Paul provides clear instruction for his listeners to follow his example of love and caring. As an imprisioned man of God, he demonstrated ministering to this church family by not requiring them to grieve over his circumstance.

We are to minister to family and love ones despite our issues in life. God understands our issues and takes care of them while we follow His directives. Let us turn our attention to a biblical story of ministering and demonstrate how this effective ministering charted a course of divine intervention.

> Now when He had ended all his sayings in the audience of the people, He entered into Capernaum. And a certain centurion's servant, who was dear unto Him, was sick, and

---

11   1 Chronicles 4:9-10

ready to die. And when he heard of Jesus, he sent unto Him the elders of the Jews, beseeching Him that he would come and heal his servant. And when they came to Jesus, they besought Him instantly, saying, That he was worthy for whom he should do this: For he loveth our nation, and he hath built us a synagogue. Then Jesus went with them. And when he was now not far from the house, the centurion sent friends to Him, saying unto Him, Lord, trouble not thyself: for I am not worthy that thou shouldest enter under my roof. Wherefore neither thought I myself worthy to come unto thee: but say in a word, and my servant shall be healed. For I also am a man set under authority, having under me soldiers, and I say unto one, Go, and he goeth; and to another, Come, and he cometh; and to my servant, Do this, and he doeth it. When Jesus heard these things, he marvelled at him, and turned him about, and said unto the people that followed him, I say unto you, I have not found so great faith, no, not in Israel. And they that were sent, returning to the house, found the servant whole that had been sick. (Luke 7:1-10)

This story is presented for several reasons. The centurion definitely had a need but required help in navigating the perceived system of assistance. The elders of the Jews possessed the cultural ability to address the petition to Jesus Christ. Jesus provided the answer. Many people are aware of the desired answer to the prayer; however, they desire earthly assistance. In this story, the Jewish elders represent the ones who ministered to the family in need and they petitioned Jesus for relief on behalf of the Centurion. They knew who Jesus was and knew that approaching Him would not be difficult because they were Jewish and Jesus would most certainly recognize them. Those ministering to family and love ones must possess equivalent faith in Jesus Christ in order to be effective.

Ministering should not be reserved for times of crisis. Within our families, ministering for illness prevention could change the course of many lives. While we witness the consumption of so much pork, fatty food, cholesterol laden delicacies and fried crusine, why do we hush our mouths and witness the insidious development of heart attack and strokes? Do effective ministers wait until disaster strikes before they sound the trumpet alerting that the enemy approaches? Will God hold ministers accountable for the failure to alert family and love ones about the dietary catastrophe which threatens them? It is our belief that ministry to family and love ones represent a continuum and goes beyond crisis intervention, terminal care or psychological misfortune.

The author of 2 Kings reports a story regarding Hezekiah and it is Hezekiah's response that will guide our thoughts. Although this story was offered previously, we introduce it here as a point of illustration.

In those days was Hezekiah sick unto death. And the prophet Isaiah the son of Amoz came to him, and said unto him, Thus saith the Lord, Set thine house in order; for thou shalt die, and not live.

> Then he turned his face to the wall and prayed unto the Lord, saying,
>
> I beseech thee, O Lord, remember now how I have walked before thee in truth and with a perfect heart, and have done that which is good in thy sight. And Hezekiah wept sore.
>
> (2 Kings 20:1-3)

Hezekiah reminded God of his (Hezekiah's) witness in life. "O Lord, remember now how I have walked before thee in truth and with a perfect heart and have done that which is good in they sight."

Hezekiah tells God that he has been a righteous leader, righteous person, kept the law, followed all dietary restrictions and had a personal relationship with Him. In response to Hezekiah's prayer, God changed his directive and gave Hezekiah fifteen more years of life. How many of us can emulate Hezekiah's prayer?

As effective ministers, it is a requirement that we help navigate the healthcare system and if possible, alert family and love ones in the prevention of illness or misfortune and in the promotion of healthy family relationships. We often hear dreadful stories regarding the fate of the black family. We would like to state it differently. When God is not at the center of the family, all families are in trouble. It is not a race or ethnic specific rubric! The solution does not require any psychological intervention; it requires consistent direction and intervention. Families may have multiple ministers to whom God has directed to be the chief architect of His divine will. It may be the family's physician, clergyperson, pastor, neighbor, friend or another family member.

Effective teaching about the family must be reemphasied because the visual and auditory media has gone to great lengths to redefine it. By their definition, a family is composed of anyone, tightly or loosely related, living under one or more roofs with like or different opinions holding a variety of needs, often with opposing solutions. This excellent definition of a dysfunctional family represents a recipe for disaster. Unfortunately, this family structure is usually devoid of any Bible based teaching. One or more persons may be in trouble with the legal system; many are in financial trouble and living on the fringes of society. Further, if death made a visit, they would probably be searching for a church in which to have the funeral. Does this sound familiar? How did we get away from the significant message as presented in Deuteronomy 6:4-9 ?

Hear, O Israel: The Lord our God is one Lord.

And thou shalt love the Lord thy God with all thine heart and with all thy soul, and with all thy might.

And these words, which I command thee this day, shall be in thine heart:

And thou shall teach them diligently unto thy children, and shall talk of them when thou sittest in thine house, and when thou walkest by the way, and when thou liest down, and when thou risest up. And thou shall bind them for a sign upon thine hand, and they shall be as frontlets between thine eyes. And thou shall write them upon thy posts of thy house and on thou gates.

Despite society's message, we must consistently sound the trumpet and warn the family of the downhill spirial of catastrophe that awaits them when Jesus Christ is left out of the family. The effective minister to the family must be one that also presents a message of reconciliation. Families must be brought back to God in order to maintain a cohesive family unit.

Family dysfunction also transcends the healthcare arena. These families present challenges for the medical staff, nurses and ancillary medical personnel in hospital settings. They also disrupt healthcare for many other people. The members of these families are usually noncompliant and they pay little to no attention to thier overall health and well being,

This chapter began with the story of WC illustrating effective ministry and we conclude it with an example of dysfunctional, thwarted ministerial effectiveness in the life of a hospitalized person.

TESTIMONIAL APPLICATION
The Story of an ICU Patient

As a woman frequently plagued with chest pain, hypertension and anxiety, XY was squeezed between two opinions. She always felt that she was owed more than others and that people were required to always be promptly attentive to her needs. She had been accustomed to visiting doctors, only to leave when her welcome was overextended and she felt that she was not receiving adequate attention. XY did not listen to reason or medical truths; her interest was only in receiving what she desired, regardless of whether or not it was of any benefit to her.

One particular night, chest pains sent her to the emergency room and coronary care unit. A visit from her husband created such a disturbance that security had to be called to remove him from the hospital. There was nothing that could be done for XY and she was subsequenly discharged from the hospital after she became stable and found free of heart disease or attending problems. She moved on to the next doctor and ultimately became a nonentity. At the time of this writing, her whereabouts are unknown. This is a sad story but one that is often repeated. Some people can be helped; however, many seek medical attention for personal gain and remain blind to any ministerial attention unless it feeds their agenda.

Those ministering to families and love ones must keep in mind that attention must be given to developing Christ-centered family relationsips while paying attention to illness prevention. If these two things are given appropriate consideration, appropriate crisis oriented ministry promises to be the end result.

CHAPTER SEVEN

Healing Through Death

Is death really the end?

On the surface, it may appear a bit oxymoronic that healing and death would appear in the same sentence. One might ask, how can one receive healing through death? As shocking as this seems, it is true and supported by scripture. We include this material as an indication that physical life is only a small part of God's eternal plan for His believers. All too often, we become engulfed in the treasures of earth and fail to focus on the treasures of heaven. God's desire for us is that we set our affections on heavenly things, those things that cannot be corrupted by thieves and moths. Consider the following scriptural warrants that elucidate the questions presented.

What is God's view of the death of His children?

Precious in the sight of the Lord is the death of His saints. (Psalm 116:15)

He will redeem their life from oppression and violence; and precious shall be their blood in His sight. (Psalm 72:14)

Then I heard a voice from heaven saying to me, "Write: Blessed are the dead who die in the Lord from now on." "Yes says the Spirit, "that they may rest from their labors, and their works follow them." (Revelation 14:13)

What does the Scripture state about death, its timelessness, purpose, and truth?

To everything there is a season, a time for every purpose under heaven: A time to be born and a time to die; a time to plant, and a time to pluck what is planted:
(Ecclesiastes 3:1, 2)

For since by man came death, by Man also came the resurrection of the dead. For as in Adam all die, even so in Christ all shall be made alive, but each one in his own order. Christ the first fruits, afterward those who are Christ's at His coming.
(1 Corinthians 15:21-22)

There remains therefore a rest for the people of God. For he who has entered His rest was himself also ceased from his works as God did from His. (Hebrews 4:9-10)

Man who is born of woman is of few days and full of trouble. He comes forth like a flower and fades away; he flees like a shadow and does not continue. (Job 14:1-2)

For there is hope for a tree, if it is cut down, that it will sprout again, and that its tender shoots will not cease...But man dies and is laid away; indeed he breaths his last and where is he? As water disappears from the sea, and a river becomes parched and dries up, so man lies down and does not rise, till the heavens are no more, they will not awake nor be roused from their sleep.

If a man dies, shall he live again? All the days of my hard service I will wait, till m change comes.
(Job 14:7, 10-12, 14)

Is physical death a necessary event?

Now this I say, brethren, that flesh and blood cannot inherit the kingdom of God; nor does corruption inherit incorruption. Behold I tell you a mystery: We shall not all sleep, but we shall all be changed.
(1 Corinthians 15:50-51)
But we all, with unveiled face, beholding as in a mirror the glory of the Lord, are being transformed into the same image from glory to glory, just as by the Spirit of the Lord.
(2 Corinthians 3:18)

Is it wrong to feel like you are ready for death when the time is near?

For we know that if our earthly house, this tent, is destroyed, we have a building from God, a house not made with hands, eternal in the heavens. For in this we groan, earnestly desiring to be clothed with our habitation, which is from heaven.

If indeed, having been clothed, we shall not be found naked. For we who are in this tent groan, being burdened, not because we want to be unclothed, but further clothed, that mortality may be swallowed up by life. (2 Corinthians 5:1-4)

For I am already being poured out as a drink offering and the time of my departure is at hand. I have fought the good fight; I have finished the race; I have kept the faith. Finally, there is laid up for me the crown for righteousness, which the Lord, the righteous Judge will give to me on that day and not to me only but also to all who have loved His appearing. (2 Timothy 4:6-8)

For I know that this will turn out for my deliverance through your prayer and the supply of the Spirit of Jesus Christ, according to my earnest expectation and hope that in nothing I shall be ashamed, but with all boldness, as always, so now also Christ will be magnified in my body, whether by life or by death. For to me, to live is Christ and to die is gain. But if I live on in the flesh, this will mean fruit from my labor; yet what I choose I cannot tell. For I am hard pressed between the two, having a desire to depart and be with Christ, which is far better.

Nevertheless to remain in the flesh is more needful for you. (Philippians 1:19-25)

For all our days have passed away in your wrath; we finish our years like a sigh.

The days of our lives are seventy years; and if by reason of strength they are eighty years, yet their boast is only labor and sorrow; for it is soon cut off, and we fly away. Who knows the power of your anger? For as the fear of you, so is Your wrath. So teach us to number our days that we may gain a heart of wisdom. (Psalm 90:9-12)

All of the scriptures that we have presented in this chapter underscore the inevitability of death and the fact that in the sight of God, death is a precious relief from life. Does this address our chapter's quest, "Healing through death?" We submit that it does; however, our task in this chapter is not yet complete.

The primary focus of this chapter is centered on the Christian's inevitable understanding that all life is eventually swallowed up in death. If this truth is accepted, then it logically follows that the eternal requiem with God does not begin until death occurs. According to 1 Corinthians 3:18, we are all being changed from glory to glory as by the Holy Spirit, into the image of Christ. The meaning of this verse rests with the fact that we will be like Him upon the day of His return, but while on earth, in this fleshly tent, we are being steadily changed into His image and likeness.

All in the flesh will suffer an eventual death; however, until that time comes, God empowers our lives and maintains us until we receive His divine call and are transformed from death to eternal life with him. Healing therefore is not spiritual but physical and that is the only way that we can understand this chapter's impact. When one prays for healing, the prayer request is usually that the physical malady be relieved, controlled, ameliorated, or removed.

The healing which God affords by physical death is that of which Scripture speaks. Healing comes in the form of eternal relief from the fleshly issues; we receive eternal rest until Jesus' return and no longer are concerned about the toils and vicissitudes of life. Healing through death ushers an eternal requiem that is only understood by God.

TESTIMONIAL APPLICATION
A Memorable Patient
(as told by Dr. Betton)

I had the fortunate opportunity to care for a brave, spirit-filled woman dying from cancer of the breast. I examined her initially and sent her for the necessary consultations, followed by surgery, chemotherapy and radiation therapy. Our conversations were replete with spiritual jargon mixed with the reality of her condition. I will never forget my final meeting with her. It was 5:15 am, while still dark outside on my daily rounding schedule. I presented to her bedside in my usual manner, greeted her, and as our eyes met each other for what we both knew would be the last time, I opened my mouth and spoke these words: "Mrs. B your soul is not sick. Your body is besieged with cancer; however, it is not your body that the Lord will receive. I want you to know that your body will not be with Him. I want you to concentrate on the fact that when your journey is complete, there does await a crown of glory for you. Hang in there!" After these words, I left her bedside and completed my hospital rounds. Mrs. B died that day and I am personally thankful to God that He allowed me to have this final chat with her.

This wonderful lady was healed by death. The body returns to the ground and the soul to God who gave it (Eccl. 12:7) and according to Paul's letter to the Corinthians, [her] mortality put on immortality and her corruptible put on incorruption. These represent healing images for Mrs. B because her citizenship was in Heaven and not on earth.

CHAPTER EIGHT

Preparing for the Transition: Accepting God's Will

What is the role of submission in the dying process?

While we felt it necessary to include this chapter, no one really knows this subject unless the individual has actually experienced and completed the transition. However, broaching this information remains very important. For those of us who are in Christ Jesus, it is important to reside in the peace that accompanies eternal life. King Solomon wrote, "The dust will return to the earth as it was and the spirit will return to God who gave it.[12]" It is important to recognize that our mortal bodies will remain here; from dust we came and to dust we shall return. Our souls shall reign with the Lord. This everlasting union of soul and spirit can only be accomplished by living a life that is pleasing unto God.

As we prepare for the transition from our earthly domain to our heavenly return, it is important to meditate upon the goodness of God and His eternal provision. In addition to medical related concerns of comfort, including living wills and advance directives, soul preparation should also have a place of priority. Additionally,

---

12 Eccl 12:7

prayer, meditation, scripture nourishment and family fellowship are also important. The period of time between the last days on earth and the time of transition should hopefully allow for sufficient time to say "good bye" and leave our families with any last wishes, words of wisdom or directions.

We present this information as physician/preacher and preacher/ attorney. As a physician/preacher who has practiced for thirty-three years, Dr. Betton has had innumerable experiences in presenting bad news. As preacher/attorney for more than twenty years, Dr. Hodges has been repeatedly called to minister to various persons after they have received bad news. Dr. Betton takes the position that the best way to convey bad news is merely to present the facts in a compassionate manner. It has been his experience that most patients prefer to know what is wrong with them without the addition of "sugar-coated information." Accordingly, we feel that it is important for the facts to be presented in a caring and professional manner that fully embraces the art and science of care giving.

Neither the physician practitioner nor the clergyperson is aware of how the patient will receive the information; however, both must be prepared to follow through with the kind of support that is helpful, educational, and empowering. We present this chapter to elucidate some of the nuances associated with managing bad news. We present the following scripture as a point of entry.

And it shall come to pass that before they call I will answer and while they are still speaking I will hear (Isaiah 65:24)

The practitioner sharing unexpected information must be prepared to deliver it just as the patient must be prepared to receive it. In both instances, God remains at work in the process. Quite often, the one who delivers the information may not have a keen knowledge of the patient. In the healthcare setting, he/she may be a consultant in a hospital setting where the diagnosis was made. In a parish setting, the minister may be called to the home of the patient to be present and provide support as the news is given. Sometimes, this information is shared without the presence of family, pastoral counselor, or clergy, or the primary care physician. When these instances occur, the outcome can be devastating for the patient.

We submit that it is crucial for the deliverer of unexpected news to communicate, when possible, with available family members before the delivery occurs. In the absence of family, a clergy professional is always a welcomed asset. In emergency situations where the clinician is the only person present, it is always recommended that an appeal is made to the staff of the Social Work department to offer assistance. Whether alone with the patient or in the presence of other supporting persons, we offer the following scripture, which we believe is a source of comfort.

> Let us therefore come boldly to the throne of grace that we may obtain mercy and find grace to help in time of need. (Hebrews 4:16)

Once the news has been shared, prayer is in order. Only through God's grace and mercy can a family adequately digest bad news and go forward with that information to its conclusion. Even though the family may be in a quandary and uncertain as to the direction of their prayer, God remains all knowing and is ever present to meet our needs even when we fail to express them.

As clergy, we certainly will pray that God's will for that person's life be manifested. In addition, we pray for God's healing powers to come to play and that the person will respond positively in any intervention suggested and agreed upon by the patient and his or her family.

> Let us therefore be diligent to enter that rest, lest anyone fall according to the same example of disobedience. (Hebrews 4:11)

The recipient of unexpected news must remember to remain in God's rest and not to make rash decisions that may be contrary to his or her health. God's rest permits one to "give way" to God's will and follow His lead. By prayer and meditation, with thanksgiving we are to make our requests known to God (Philippians 4:6). In this sphere of rest, one is able to prioritize his/her spiritual affairs. For the one who has accepted the Lord Jesus Christ as his/her personal Savior, this is an easy assignment.

Unexpected news does not necessarily consign the patient to a death sentence. It confronts them with their humanity, their life on earth and their eternal position in Christ. The recipient of unexpected news is often faced with the terminality of it and may translate it into such statements as whether they will defeat the cancer, end-stage heart, lung, liver, or other organ disease. They may feel badly as they go through the therapies; the medication may send them through the "valley of the shadow of death;" and they may even feel like giving up. Somewhere during their journey, they may share with someone that "they are tired" and ready to go home to be with the Lord. These expressions are perfectly acceptable and should be appreciated by the listeners. It is during these times that the care giver must be supportive of clinical treatment, while simultaneously embracing the patient's desire for eternal rest. Consider the following scripture:

> And my God shall supply all your needs according to His riches in glory by Christ Jesus. (Philippians 4:19)

The care giver's role is to comfort and attend to the physical needs of the person while compassionately giving attention to his/her mental health needs. In this realm, prayer, spiritual meditation and Bible reading become paramount. Although we may not often think about it, the sick, infirmed and terminally ill appreciate prayer, scripture and opportunities for meditation. These individuals are usually unable to attend church and receive a corporate worship experience; yet they have a craving for the word of God to minister to their souls. The care giver, church members, neighbors and others in attendance can provide this necessary service. We present the following testimony as an excellent witness of coping with bad news while continuing to exercise sincere faith in and commitment to God's word.

TESTIMONIAL APPLICATION
Testimony of John Gordon, M.D.
(as told by Dr. Gordon)

When one gives a testimony, you must try to remember the goal in mind and the essence of the story. What I hope to do is tell how God in His divine timing and wisdom is giving me an exciting adventure about what really should be important in my life. Prior to the onset of this adventure, I was relatively healthy except for the occasional aches in my shoulders, legs and lower back, which I attributed to being a paratrooper while in the military. My spiritual life was improving, while I found more time to read God's Word and settle in a church with good fellowship. Basically, I considered myself spiritually mature, blessed with a beautiful wife, five children and a very promising career in anesthesiology. I stayed very active physically and professionally until June 2000. The only medical concern I had at this time was swelling in my lower extremities with prolonged standing, an occasional night sweats and increased tiredness, which I attributed to working long hours. I had also noticed some difficulty when attempting to climb the hospital stairwells anywhere from 3 to 6 floors to perform my daily rounds on patients. My routine annual physical was normal except for unexplained peripheral edema of the lower extremities as explained above and this was attributed to protein breakdown from my exercising. I ate healthy and exercised by either jogging or playing tennis at least twice a week.

On the morning of June 23rd, 2000 while I was providing anesthesia, an operating room nurse commented on how "bad" I looked, "as if you're ill." After trying to ignore her comment, she convinced me to have some lab work done "just for curiosity." Approximately two hours later, I received lab values that I knew could not have been mine; they revealed severe anemia.

I decided to submit another sample later that afternoon and it confirmed that I was indeed, severely anemic. So what would most intelligent physicians do when faced with a medical problem? You're right; I decided to be my own doctor and rule out the most likely causes of anemia, gastrointestinal bleeding from the high anti-inflammatory agents I was taking for my general body aches. Since I felt that my condition was a result of the high dosage of medications, I tapered my dosage and decided to observe my stools for occult bleeding. After several weeks of playing around with being my own doctor, I decided to get serious and seek the Lord with this dilemma.

On Monday, July 17th while spending time in my early morning prayer, the Holy Spirit revealed to me that I had cancer and it was Multiple Myeloma. I had no anxiety with this new revelation; instead, I had a peace beyond my understanding. That morning while at work, I called a friend whose specialty was Hematology/Oncology and he suggested that I submit some more blood for labs, obtain a total body CT scan and have a bone marrow biopsy which he was willing to perform on Thursday 20th.

After having the biopsy done, I sat in my car before going home and prayed, asking God to give me the strength and ability to give Him honor and glory no matter what the final diagnosis revealed. It was ten days before I got the news; however, as I previously indicated, the Holy Spirit had prepared me for the news that I would receive.

I continued to work as if nothing was wrong and the nurse, who made the observation about my health, honored my request of keeping the information about the anemia confidential. I finally decided to prepare my wife for the bad news, so Sunday, July 23rd I informed her I probably had some type of cancer. As she cried, she said, "I know." We decided to pray together as always and give this over to God and seek His direction on treatment and when to tell the rest of the family.

It was not until July 28th when my oncologist friend informed me with tears in his eyes that I indeed had cancer, a Non Hodgkin's Lymphoma with widespread involvement, making me stage 4 class B. He also informed me that I should start treatment that following Monday. I asked him my prognosis and he replied 18 months to three years. I arranged my schedule so that I could receive chemotherapy during the day and take my routine call in the operating room at night. This way none of my partners needed to know about my treatment. However after four days of treatment, I was feeling tired and had an episode of diffuse sweating with dizziness and had to be relieved by one of my closest friends, in whom I confided about my illness.

The next morning on August the 4th I decided that giving anything less than my best would not constitute the standards of care I so much endorsed, so I decided to resign.

At the time of my resignation, I was at the pinnacle of my career; President of our anesthesia group; I held a very prestigious appointment on the hospital's executive board and I was Chairman of a nearby surgery center. In the back of my mind, I wondered, why now God, only to remember the prayer I had prayed several years ago, "do whatever it takes Lord to make me see and do Your will." I pause briefly to suggest that you be careful what you pray for!

On August 9th of 2000, I had a discussion with my wife and reminded her that I knew I was called into the Gospel ministry during my early 20's and this was confirmed by scripture laid on my heart, dreams and even comments that strangers would make, but I refused to yield to God's calling. At this point, I felt that my health was dependent on me being obedient to what God had called me to do. She agreed and said she would be supportive in whatever way possible. Some of my immediate concerns were the debt I would leave for my wife and family, if the Lord decided to take me home and how best to prepare my children to live a life without me.

I decided to sell the 10,000 sq ft. dream home we had built and had enjoyed for the last 10 years and also to decrease all other debt as quickly as possible. After much prayer, we gradually informed the children and encouraged them to draw closer to God during this time for a peace only He could give them. Chemotherapy was taking a toll on my body, with frequent aches, chills and fevers, which kept me pretty much homebound.

Toward the end of August, I was waiting for my son somewhere (I do not recall) when my eyes fell upon a July 2000 Reader's Digest. The front page was about a CEO of a start-up biotech company, who invented a Stem Cell purification system that later was used to treat himself for Lymphoma. At this time this was just an interesting article and still something on the cutting edge of medicine, but it remained on my mind.

I was under the impression that my treatment was having a positive effect on the cancer since I had daily treatment for nearly a month. However, on September 21st, my oncology friend informed me that I needed to transfer my care to the University of Maryland and all the necessary paperwork was already done. I would be lying if I said I did not feel somewhat depressed and surprised, so once more I prayed that God would continue to give me strength and direction with the type of treatment I should have at this time. It just so happened, those 9 days later during my quiet time, I read something by Oswald Chambers "how one must not run from preaching the Gospel and not complain about the hands or circumstances that God may use to prepare you."

I was scheduled for my first appointment with the head of the lymphoma unit on August 31, 2000. My friend (oncologist) and I both agreed that treatment within the Greenebaum Cancer Center (GBCC) would be more beneficial since little progress was being made at that time with the present treatment plan of Fludarabine and Rutuximab. I had further diagnostic workups at the GBCC and eventually was treated with Cyclophosphamide and Etoposide during October 2000 with the intent of having a stem cell transplant (SCT) in the near future.

In the process of preparing for the transplant, I expressed my concerns about the fact that my IgA and IgM (cancer markers) were still significantly elevated and whether this would cause me to go into early relapse? As time progressed, I prayed to know if this was the right thing to do or if I should investigate other treatment modalities. While waiting for some type of direction from the Holy Spirit, I decided to talk with patients who recently underwent transplants. I learned not only about the successful transplants but also the terrible relapses and cases where patients had expired during the process.

One night while I was waiting to receive the next phase in the transplant procedure, I got a strong feeling that I should leave the hospital. After praying and trying to get peace on this matter, I decided that it was best for me to leave. I informed the transplant team that I wanted to leave; this behavior was extremely dangerous since I was in a compromised immune state. The doctors finally acquiesced to discharge me once I signed the papers releasing the hospital/doctors from liability since this was against medical advice. After reassuring my wife that I was not trying to get away from her by committing medical suicide, I remained in isolation until my immune status was back to normal.

On January 16th 2001, I decided to pursue a desire that had been on my heart for more than twenty years, I registered in Capital Bible Seminary with the plan of getting well or dying learning God's Word. At the time of this decision my wife had legitimate financial concerns since we were now on a fixed budget and school would be an additional expense. Within my heart, I knew this was what God wanted me to do and some way it would all work out if we would just trust Him. My first class started on January 23rd; the atmosphere and teaching that day confirmed that I was indeed in the right place. My health was stable. Except for the same body aches and pain from the neuropathy, I was now in Heaven on earth. Suddenly, I realized that I was "old," the students around me were the age of my kids and many of them referred to me as "the old man" in a positive way. It did my heart well that God was giving me another chance to get on board with His plan for my life. I often observed with a smile, the young men and women around me at Seminary and wondered what adventures God had in store for them.

At the end of January 2001, the University of Maryland Oncology Department, asked if I wanted to be in a non FDA evaluation of a new drug called Zevalin. After much prayer, I consented to receive this experimental drug. For the next six months, things were far from just routine labs and CT scans. We were always dealing with some type of drama with our children either during high school and college basketball games or among the older sibling in law school. There seemed to never be a dull moment. My wife and I were also a target of a house selling scam that revealed scandalous characters, the same kind of stuff you see on the program "Sixty Minutes." All of the players were eventually reported to the police. One of the highlights of the summer occurred on Monday August 27, 2001 when we got a contract to sell our home after it had been on the market for nearly a year with multiple brokers.

The other highlight was a supernatural one and it occurred on August 28th. I had just found out that a doctor at MD Anderson, who specialized in rare lymphomas, would not be able to see me. This was a surprise since I had a positive conversation with him just three weeks prior and this conversation focused on how to send my medical records. So, somewhat confused and depressed I decided to go for a walk and clear my head. We were staying in an apartment while our house was on the market, so I walked to the apartment complex exercise room. Normally at night there is no one there; however on this particular night, there were two white females who appeared to be in their mid to late twenties. I figured they would leave as soon as I arrived since the room was approximately 20x20 with only four pieces of equipment, some free weights and a television.

Surprisingly, the young women continued to talk with each other. It was virtually impossible not to hear their conversation. By this time I just wanted them to leave so I could change the television to ESPN. I eventually invited myself into their conversation, when one of them said "God has laid something on my heart and I don't know what to do about it." I interjected, "have you prayed about it and you may even need to find time for a fast." She welcomed my response and said to her friend, "I told you he must be a Christian." At this point, she tried to explain this "weird feeling" she had experienced over the last two weeks by stating, "this is not pertaining to my husband or son and nobody in my family is ill." She continued by saying, "I have the feeling that I am to talk to someone who has cancer or something." At this point I started to have chills and my legs began to buckle while I was on the treadmill. Both of them noticed that I was deeply affected by her comment so she asked, "What's wrong?"

At this point, I informed her that I had cancer and was just informed that the doctor I was waiting to see could not see me and did not offer an explanation. With this she screamed, "it's you, oh my God, you're the one God wants me to tell everything is going to be alright, don't worry, you have the Doctor of the Universe and you're healed." I was so startled at this point that I could not contain my emotions. I burst into tears only to be hugged by both of them as we jumped up and down praising God.

After the excitement, Sara and Christy, my newfound friends, came back to my apartment and shared this good news with my wife who also was astonished. Not that I had any doubt in what God could do but to convey a message to me from an absolute stranger was once more revealing the fact that He is a God that hears our prayers and knows the concerns of our heart. From that point on, I never picked up the burden of my health again; my healing was all in God's time and His way.

The confirmation of this supernatural event occurred approximately three weeks later when I was assisting my daughter in buying a car. After test driving the vehicle and deciding this was the car, my daughter proceeded to take care of the paper work. The salesman treated us with a tank of gas. Once arriving back at the dealership, the salesman's associate stated how they had been looking for the salesman. She then looked over at me, came to the driver's side, placed her hand on my arm, and said "Have you been sick?" I stated, "I don't know how to answer that question." Her reply was, "don't worry brother; you are going to be healed." I started tearing up and told both of them they had no idea of the things that had happened to me. I then thanked them for their encouragement. I later found out that my daughter had not said anything to anyone at the dealership concerning my health.

The next eight years were filled with many dark roads and deep valleys. The treatments were many consisting of various types of chemotherapy: Rituxan, Velcade, Revlimid, Thalidomide, Doxil and some I do not even remember. I never lost hope and the Lord sustained me through seminary, along with multiple hospital and ICU admissions for congestive heart failure, pneumonia, renal insufficiency, GI bleeding and fever of uncertain or unknown causes. Each new oncologist would say "you've beat the odds, and you look fairly strong and healthy considering the disease." I often looked to use this as an opportunity to comment on the awesome God that I served and how I came to know Him through Jesus Christ. I would elaborate on how the "disease" was really a blessing; it helped me to leave medicine in good standing and spend more time with my family. It also drew my entire family closer to God.

My cancer markers were very inconsistent with increases ranging from 1-15 % a year until September 2009. At that time, my oncologist stated he had some bad news: "not only are your lymphoma markers steadily increasing, but you also have evidence of Multiple Myeloma." At this time in my walk with God I had peace no matter what my colleagues told me, I just thought to myself "God and I are going to have a wild adventure together." I consulted with various oncology centers: University of North Carolina, Chapel Hill; University Medical Center, Arizona; University of Maryland; Johns Hopkins and Dana Farber of Harvard University.

After multiple bone biopsies, labs and skeletal surveys, it was confirmed that I had two cancers: the Non Hodgkin's Lymphoma and Multiple Myeloma. Several different oncology teams gave me a dismal prognosis, leaving a stem cell transplant as the only option. This was starting to sound like a repeat conversation of ten years ago "stem cell transplant is your only hope" but the difference was that I had peace and was actually looking forward to have the procedure done.

My wife and I sought the will of God and after having peace with the decision to proceed; we contacted everyone we knew for prayer intervention. After having several months of pre transplant chemotherapy, which caused severe neuropathy in my hands and feet, I entered the University of Maryland; the date was January 2010. I had my transplant on January 15th and my stay at the hospital went exceptionally well.

I had so many people praying for me that God probably got tired of getting the petitions. I had no complications or side effects and was discharged from the hospital approximately 10 days early and from the safe house two weeks early. My stamina and mindset stayed strong and for this, I give all the glory and honor to God. As of April 28, 2010, I have been informed that I am cancer free, praise God!

In closing, I would only add that this was a very condensed story highlighting how my Heavenly Father used an illness to weave a beautiful and meaningful adventure which I am certain, is not over. I anticipate that there will be new twists but I know that my faith has been strengthened and my heart has been encouraged. I have no option but to share the goodness of God with others so that they too will know and understand that "it is not over until God says that it is over!" Meditating Scriptures:

While few testimonies will provide the level of detail as given by Dr. Gordon, we believe that the essence of his message clearly explains the importance of accepting God's will. We offer the following scriptures to encourage those who may be caregivers for others who have received bad news. These scriptures may easily be used as a source of comfort to the patient, clinician and/or minister.

I have fought the good fight, I have finished the race, I have kept the faith.

Finally, there is laid up for me the crown of righteousness, which the Lord, the righteous Judge, will give to me on that Day, and not to me only but also to all who have loved His appearing. (2 Timothy 4: 7-8)

Then the King will say to those on His right hand, 'Come, you blessed of My Father, inherit the kingdom prepared for you from the foundation of the world: for I was hungry and you gave Me food; I was thirsty and you gave Me drink; I was a stranger and you took Me in; I was naked and you clothed Me; I was sick and you visited Me; I was in prison and you came to Me.' (Matthew 25:34-35)

Father, I desire that they also whom You gave Me may be with Me where I am, that they may behold My glory which you have given Me; for You loved Me before the foundation of the world. (John 17:24)

For I am persuaded that neither death nor life, nor angels nor principalities nor powers, nor things present nor things to come, nor height nor depth, nor any other created thing, shall be able to separate us from the love of God which is in Christ Jesus our Lord. (Romans 8:38-39)

I have been young, and now am old; Yet I have not seen the righteous forsaken, nor his descendants begging bread. (Psalm 37:25)

Now this I say, brethren, that flesh and blood cannot inherit the kingdom of God; nor does corruption inherit incorruption. Behold, I tell you a mystery: We shall not all sleep, but we shall all be changed

– in a moment, in the twinkling of an eye, at the last trumpet. For the trumpet will sound, and the dead will be raised incorruptible, and this mortal must put on immortality. So when this corruptible has put on incorruption, and this mortal has put on immortality, then shall be brought to pass the saying that is written: "Death is swallowed up in victory." O death, where is your sting? O Hades, where is your victory?" The sting of death is sin, and the strength of sin is the law. But thanks be to God, who give us the victory through our Lord Jesus Christ. Therefore, my beloved brethren, be steadfast, immovable, always abounding in the work of the Lord, knowing that your labor is not in vain in the Lord. (I Corinthians 15:50-58)

And God will wipe away every tear from their eyes; there shall be no more death, nor sorrow, nor crying. There shall be no more pain, for the former things have passed away. (Revelation 21:4)

They shall see His face, and His name shall be on their foreheads. There shall be no night there: They need no lamp nor light of the sun, for the Lord God gives them light. And they shall reign forever and ever. (Revelation 22:4-5)

Blessed are those who do His commandments, that they may have the right to the tree of life, and may enter though the gates into the city. (Revelation 22:14)

Epilogue

This book represents the third in a series of books devoted to the subject of spirituality and medicine. Our first book, ***Spirituality and Medicine: Can the Two Walk Together?***, presented a summary of Howard University Hospital's 10-year preamble into this subject. In addition to the science that supports the union of spirituality and medicine, our first book offered numerous testimonies supporting scientific observations.

Our second book, ***Translating Spirituality and Medicine in the Healing Professions: A Physician-Clergy Handbook***, was devoted to techniques and tools to utilize the connection of spirituality and medicine at the bedside of the patient. While offered as an easy to read manual, it can also be viewed as a prayer book, a pocket tool for physicians, clergy and the laity to use at the bedside when offering spiritual instruction or counseling to one in need. It was designed to be a ready-resource or compendium of scripture and testimonies that can be shared to encourage the infirmed person as well as the one who is being used by God as an instrument/agent of healing.

While we recognize that this third presentation does not present the conclusion of the matter, we believe that it is useful as a resource. It provides poignant scripture references and testimonies addressing areas that are infrequently discussed. Oftentimes believers will intentionally avoid conversations regarding praying according to the will of God, spiritualizing illness or healing through death. We do not suggest that our opinions and positions are ultimate authority; however, we offer God's word to settle those areas where some would rather not engage in discussion. It is our prayer that this book provides comfort and encouragement as it draws you closer to the source of all healing, our Lord and Savior Jesus the Christ. We will continue to listen to the voice of the Lord as we delve further into the mysterious connection between spirituality and medicine. To you our readers, we say, remain encouraged and connected to the divine healer. He is able to keep you from falling!

Index of Scriptures and Topics

Chapter One

Health and Wellness: The Primacy of Health
and the Prevention of Illness
Does God require us to keep our bodies healthy?

Chapter Two
Health and Wellness: The Restorative Power of Meditation and Prayer
Does prayer really work?

Confidence in prayer:	Job 42:8; Isaiah 65:24; Jeremiah 42:2; Matthew 5:44; Mark 11:23-24; John 14:13-14; Thessalonians 3:1; 2; Hebrews 4:16; James 5:16; 1 John 5:14-15
Meditation:	Genesis 24:63; Joshua 1:8; Psalm 1:1-2; 19:14; 119:97

Chapter Three
Coping with Life's challenges
Does faith in God enable one to cope with illness?

The temple of God:	1 Corinthians 3:16-17
Mental tranquility:	Proverbs 9:10-11; 11:14; 12:26; Psalm 1:1-3; 139:13-16; Isaiah 26:3; Matthew 5:1-11; Luke 10:41-42; Philippians 4:6-7
Healing narratives:	Mark 5:1-2, 6-8, 8-19; 10:46-49, 52; Luke 17:11-19; John 5:6-9
Dealing with affliction:	Psalm 22:23, 24; 25:16-18; 34:19; 102:1-4; 119:50, 66-68, 71, 107; Matthew 6:11, 25a, 31-34; James 5:13-16

Coping with illness:	Isaiah 65:24; 65:12-13; Jeremiah16:19a; 17:14-15; 33:3; Psalm 34:1-3, 15; 37:25; 119:50
The terminally ill:	Psalm 90:10, 12, 14, 15a; 116:15; Ecclesiastes 12:7; Matthew 25:34; John 14:1-3; 17:20-24; 1 Corinthians 15: 50-54, 58; 1 Thessalonians 4:16-18; 2 Timothy 4:7-8; Revelation 22:14, 16-17

Chapter Four
The Fallacy of Spiritualizing Illness
What is spiritual healing?

Healing for wholeness:	John 5:1-14
Ready for a healing:	Matthew 9:2-7; 17:14-21; Luke 8:43-48
Healing by divine intent:	Luke 13:11-13

Chapter Five
Praying according to the Will of God
How is one to determine the will of God?

Praying responsibly:	Mark 11:23-24; John 14:13-14; Hebrews 4:16; 1 John 2:15-16; 5:14-15

Inescapable truths:	Isaiah 26:3; John 4:14; 8:31, 51; 14:1-4; 16:22, 23, 33; 17:15-17; Romans 8:26, 29-30; Galatians 5:1; Colossians 2:14
Praying specifically:	Genesis 8:20-21; Exodus 3:7-9; 1 Samuel 1:8-11, 19-20; Matthew 6:5-13
God's will for believers:	Isaiah 38:1-5; John 10:10; 15:4-8; 17:20-26

Chapter Six

Ministering to Family and Love Ones

Does ministering to family members ever present a challenge?

What God says:	Matthew 5:3,6; Philippians 4:6-7
Navigating the healthcare system:	2 Kings 20: 1-3; Luke 7:1-10
Crisis prevention:	Deuteronomy 6:4-9

Chapter Seven
Healing Through Death
Is death really the end?

What God says about death: Job 14:1,2,7,10-12,14; Psalm 72:14; 90:9-12; 116:15; Ecclesiastes 3:1,2; 1 Corinthians 15:21-22, 50, 51; 2 Corinthians 3:18; 5:1-4; Philippians 1:19-25; 2 Timothy 4:6-8; Hebrews 4:9-10; Revelation 14:13

Chapter Eight
Preparing for the Transition: Accepting God's Will
What is the role of submission in the dying process?

Sharing bad news: Hebrews 4:11, 16; Philippians 4:19

Comforting scriptures: Psalm 37:25; Matthew 25:34, 35; John 17:24; Romans 8:38, 39; 1 Corinthians 15:50-58; 2 Timothy 4:7, 8; Revelation 22:4, 5, 14